Charlemagne

A dynamic portrait of the leading ruler of medieval times, who became defender of Christendom by defeating Rome's enemies and establishing the Church in the lands he conquered. During the forty-seven years Charlemagne ruled almost all of Europe, he instituted forms of self-government and other reforms that unified his extensive empire. He encouraged the building of roads and bridges, and set up a uniform system of money, weights and measures. To insure justice for all, he codified the laws of the countries he conquered. A man of great learning, he was interested in educating his people—establishing schools and encouraging the preservation of classical literature so that knowledge of the ancient world would endure. Charlemagne's reign of enlightenment marked a civilizing influence on a Europe steeped in darkness and chaos.

Books by MANUEL KOMROFF

CHARLEMAGNE
DISRAELI
THOMAS JEFFERSON
NAPOLEON
MARCO POLO
JULIUS CAESAR

Charlemagne

by
Manuel Komroff

Julian Messner, Inc.
New York

Published by Julian Messner, Inc.
8 West 40 Street, New York 18

Printed in the United States of America
Library of Congress Catalog Card No. 64–20149

Acknowledgment

Historically the early Middle Ages are shrouded in mystery. The period is involved and torn by forces which only in recent years have been partially explored by scholars of history. The vast research and organization required for this slim volume would not have been possible without the assistance of my wife, Odette Komroff, who also shared in the writing of this book.

M. K.

1/8/65   me al

c. 1

Contents

Contents

Charlemagne

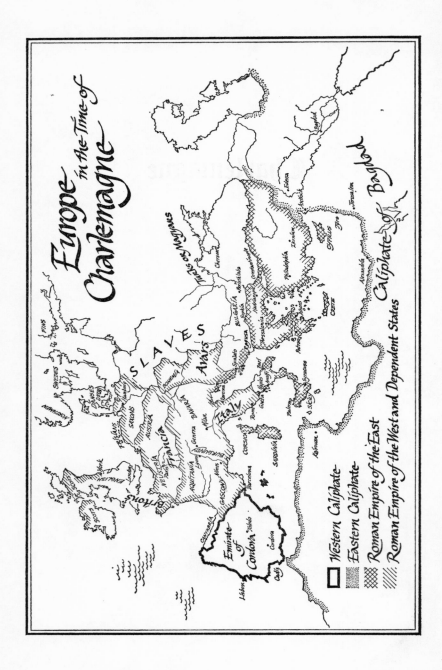

Europe in the Time of Charlemagne

Western Caliphate

Eastern Caliphate

Roman Empire of the East

Roman Empire of the West and Dependent States

1

The Three Kings of the Franks

Charlemagne, the greatest of all medieval kings, was only eleven years old when he first stepped upon the stage of history. He was the elder of two sons of Pepin the Short, King of the Franks, and the ancient chronicles first mention him as escorting Pope Stephen II into his father's realm during the first week of January in the year 754.

The aged Pope had left Rome and journeyed into Frankland under the most difficult circumstances. Riding on horseback and escorted by only a small retinue, His Holiness had crossed the treacherous Alps in the bitter month of November. To honor the Vicar of St. Peter, Pepin sent young Charles with a small company of nobles to meet him on the road and escort him back to the royal palace at Ponthion, some miles east of Paris.

Young Charles had been brought up in a very religious home. His mother, Queen Bertrada, a pious woman, and the Abbé Fulrad of St. Denis, one of the most distinguished and learned men of Gaul, had imbued young Charles with a deep love of God. And so it was undoubtedly with a full sense of reverence that he undertook his mission.

Dressed in the simple but colorful fashion of the Franks —coarse linen breeches, a short fringed tunic of yellow, red, blue or green, bright-colored woolen stockings laced with bands of a contrasting color, shoes of soft leather and a long fur cape clasped over the right shoulder—he rode southeast on the road that led to St. Maurice in the heart of the Alps. It was there that the Pope had been resting from the hardships of the first part of his trip, and it was from there, messengers reported, he had started out a few days back on the last lap of his journey.

After traveling for many long hours, young Charles finally saw the Pope's procession approaching from the distance. As the two parties drew nearer, Charles halted his little band and ordered that all dismount. Then walking timidly forward a few paces, he waited.

As the Pope and his retinue drew closer the boy beheld

a sight dazzling and glorious beyond belief. It was magnificent, different from anything that young Charles, brought up in the crude and primitive Frankish kingdom, had ever before seen. The Pope was attired in the vestments of his high office. Over his full white silk robe he wore a stole of heavy cloth woven of pure gold threads. Over this he wore a sleeveless outer vestment of richly embroidered blue silk. The trappings of his horse, the bridle and saddle, were richly ornamented. And the toes of his golden shoes rested in silver stirrups.

The boy fell to his knees as the Pope drew his horse to a halt beside him. And there under the wide blue sky he received the blessing of the Holy Father.

No pope had ever before come into the land of the Franks, and Pope Stephen had only undertaken this long and dangerous journey because of the most desperate circumstances. The King of the Lombards, descendants of a barbaric Germanic tribe which, two hundred years before, had conquered and settled all of northern Italy and some of the lands east and south of Rome, had forcefully taken lands and cities which the Pope claimed rightfully belonged to the Papacy. On top of this the King of the Lombards was demanding that Rome submit to him; if the city resisted he threatened to slaughter every inhabitant.

The Pope had appealed many times to his emperor, the Roman Emperor in Constantinople, but his pleas had been ignored. In despair, as a last resort, he had come to beg Pepin the Short to send an army against the evil Lombards.

CHARLEMAGNE

He felt that in all Europe only the King of the Franks was powerful enough to save Rome and the Papacy.

It was not often that a pope left the city of Rome to visit a far-off land; not often that a pope was forced to beg a favor from a king. Aware of this and to ease the humiliation of the living representative of St. Peter, to show his respect and loyalty, Pepin had sent Charles to meet and escort the Pope into his realm. And when His Holiness was only three miles from his palace at Ponthion, Pepin set forth with a great cavalcade of nobles to extend his personal welcome.

Humbly Pepin, King of the Franks, bowed before the Vicar of Rome. And humbly, on foot, he led the Pope's horse by the bridle the three miles back to the palace.

Pope Stephen stayed at Ponthion with King Pepin for a number of days and told him all the details of his quarrel with the King of the Lombards. But Pepin was not moved by the Pope's troubles. He did not want to become involved in a war with the Lombards far off in Italy, south of the Alps. Neither did he feel that the Pope's claims were valid. Nevertheless he finally succumbed.

However, he explained to Stephen that he could not declare war nor lead an army against the Lombards until he had received the consent of his nobles and chiefs at the great national assembly held on the first of March each year. The Field of March, as this gathering was known, had come down from ancient times; it was the survival of the intertribal assemblies of the barbaric Germans. At these

14

gatherings the king, his nobles and chieftains decided upon national problems such as trade, treason, conscription and war.

Satisfied that Pepin would live up to his promise, Pope Stephen left Ponthion and went to the Abbey of St. Denis close to Paris to recuperate from his long and trying journey. He said that he had suffered severely from "divers perils" such as floods and unbearable cold while crossing those "impossible mountains" and was in sore need of a rest.

When spring arrived the Pope was still at St. Denis enjoying the hospitality and care of the Abbé Fulrad and his monks. Pepin went to visit him there with Queen Bertrada, his sons, Charles and his younger brother Carloman, and all his court. The general assembly had agreed to an invasion of Lombardy and an army was being made ready. Pepin's promise to the Pope was being fulfilled, and the King of the Franks now wanted something in return!

Pepin and Queen Bertrada had been crowned only three years before. Boniface, that holy man from Britain who was the first to bring Christianity to the pagan Germans and who was hailed by all as a saint, had officiated. Before a great and colorful assemblage of Frankish nobles and peasants he had anointed Pepin and Bertrada with holy oil and administered an oath whereby Pepin swore to rule like a true Christian and to defend the Church against all enemies. Before this time the kings of the Franks had ruled by the consent of the people. On that day they received

15

power from the Church, and from that day on they and all the kings of Europe who were to follow for several centuries were to rule by "Divine Right."

Yes, there could be no question about it, Pepin had been duly anointed and crowned. But now he wanted the Pope to repeat the ceremony, this time including his two sons. So on July 28, 754, at St. Denis, Pepin the Short, Bertrada and the two boys were anointed by the Vicar of St. Peter, and Pepin, Charles and Carloman were proclaimed the "Three Kings of the Franks."

As an added honor Pope Stephen made them protectors of Rome by bestowing upon each of them the ancient and most honorable title of Patriarch of Rome.

In 754 Europe was for the most part covered with dense forests and dark marshes. It was in the midst of this unmapped wilderness that the kingdom of the Franks was situated. It was a large kingdom made up of the separate lands of Neustria, Burgundy, Bavaria, Alemania, Austrasia and Francia, or what we know today as northern France, the Rhone Valley, Switzerland, Bavaria, Austria, Hungary, southern Holland, the Rhine Valley and Belgium. Its inhabitants were the descendants of those barbaric tribes— such as the Goths, Huns and Vandals—which had lived there before the days of Caesar and which had only a few hundred years before swept down from the north and east destroying the Roman Empire.

THE THREE KINGS OF THE FRANKS

In Frankland, as in the rest of Europe, mountains and rivers formed almost impassable barriers between countries and tribal lands. Roads built by the Romans were few and long neglected, and although there were bridges in Italy, the rivers of Frankland and the rest of Europe could be crossed only by boats or at fords.

There were few cities north of the Alps, and most of them were situated in the southern part of Gaul outside of Frankland. All, including Paris and London, far off across the Channel, were very small, little more than towns. The rest of Europe was dotted with fortified places around which clustered the hovels, sheds and cottages of those seeking protection from the many robbers and marauding bands which roamed the countryside. These fortified places, great stone towers and stockades constructed of stout logs, were built by powerful chiefs and nobles and housed armed men.

The population of Frankland was very sparse. It has been estimated that not over thirty million people inhabited the whole vast expanse of Europe. England had less than one million people. With wars, plagues, famines and the primitive state of medicine, life expectancy was only twenty-seven years.

All men in the land of the Franks lived by tilling the soil. Merchants and peddlers were few. There was no industry. These men, with their feet in the soil, were ignorant, dull, unimaginative and superstitious, but they were not serfs. They were, for the most part, freemen and owned land or

17

worked land which was lent them by those richer. Serfdom was only beginning to come into existence, and feudalism was still far off.

There were no schools; there was little culture. While the Christian Church was firmly established in Rome and southern Gaul, it was not yet so firmly implanted in Frankland. The Franks were Christians, it is true, and their land abounded in churches, monasteries and nunneries; but in times of illness, famine and war when men were pressed harder than usual, the people looked back longingly to their old gods and consulted witches and soothsayers who were still in touch with these long-neglected deities. On the borders of Frankland were many peoples, like the Saxons and Avars, who still worshiped their ancient gods. The men to the east and north were very primitive and barbaric. It was indeed a dark age.

Life was stark and hard for the people of Frankland and the rest of Europe in the days preceding Charlemagne. And it was made still more insecure by an outside danger. The Mediterranean was no longer a "Roman lake," because during the end of the sixth century a new religion had been founded in Arabia by the Prophet Mohammed. It spread with amazing speed, taking possession of many eastern lands such as Syria and Persia and sweeping across north Africa into Spain and southern Gaul. It was Charles the Hammer, father of Pepin the Short and grandfather of the boy Charles, who at the Battle of Tours in 732 stopped the advance of these "infidels" and drove them back across the

Pyrenees into Spain, thus saving Europe for Christianity.

Yes, it was a simple Frank and not a great Roman general at the head of brave legions who had saved Europe. Although the Roman Empire still existed and all of Italy and most of Europe including the Frankish kingdom technically belonged to it, it had lost its power and meaning. The Empire had grown weak and had abandoned Europe when, in A.D. 330, Constantine the Great, the first Christian emperor, moved the capital from Rome to a new city which he had built far away on the Bosporus and which he named after himself, Constantinople.

Europe had been deserted as a result of this, and by the time Charles was born a cleavage had occurred in the Empire, a cleavage which was to grow more pronounced with the years and culminate during Charlemagne's lifetime in a complete division of the Roman Empire into two parts: the Eastern Roman Empire, or Byzantine Empire, and the Western Roman Empire.

The reluctant Pepin fulfilled his promise to the Pope. Following his coronation at St. Denis, and when his armies were ready, he crossed the Alps and invaded Lombardy. He took the Pope with him in order to insure His Holiness a safe and comfortable journey home, and it is believed that he also had little Charles in his company. In those days boys of nine and ten took part in battles, and sons of kings were experienced enough in warfare by the time they reached twelve or thirteen to be placed in charge of whole armies!

There are unfortunately no records of what part, if any, Charles played during this campaign. All we know is that the Lombards were quickly vanquished and that Pepin the Short "took much treasure of gold and silver" and dictated the terms of peace. The King of the Lombards was ordered to surrender the lands and cities which the Pope claimed were his. He was also forced to pay Pepin a large tribute and to recognize him as his lord.

The terms of this peace were generous indeed considering the time and how Pepin had been inconvenienced. It can be explained only by the fact that Pepin was still not the least bit interested in the quarrel between the Lombard King and the Pope and wanted only to be done with the whole business as quickly as possible. He did not ask for hostages or secure any other guarantees. He did not leave an army of occupation. As soon as the treaty was signed he led his army back home across the Alps, hoping that he had heard the last of the Pope's complaints.

But Pepin was too hopeful. No sooner was he home than urgent messages began to arrive from the Pope, messages filled with horrible stories about the Lombards, who it seemed had not turned over the disputed territories and were now attacking churches, raping nuns and pillaging the countryside around Rome. And so Pepin was forced to return and wage another campaign against the Lombards. This time Pepin made sure that the lands and cities which the Pope claimed would forever remain in the hands of the Papacy. Even though these lands did not belong to

Pepin—they belonged to the Roman Empire and could be disposed of only by the Emperor in Constantinople—Pepin deeded them to the Church forevermore.

Having made the "Donation of Pepin," as his gift to the Pope is known in history, Pepin now returned to Frankland confident that he would not be disturbed again. And it was so. Pepin never again had to fight for the Pope. But because of his "Donation," his son Charles, after he assumed the crown, was destined to wage several campaigns in Italy.

Having finally settled the dispute between the Pope and the Lombards, Pepin occupied himself with a matter which he liked much better. Taking Charles along to assist him, he spent the next nine years conquering the Duchy of Aquitaine, a large and rich province of southern Gaul which stretched from Nantes and Bourges in the north to the Pyrenees in the south and from the Atlantic in the west to the Auvergnes Mountains in the east. The Duchy of Aquitaine was the last stronghold in Europe of Roman culture. Here, even more than in Italy itself, one found the living remains of Roman literature, architecture, medicine, art and music—a cultural heritage which appears to have exerted a deep influence on young Charles, who during the years he served in this war was growing into manhood.

It is believed that Aquitaine influenced Charles this way because of his lifetime interest in all cultural matters, but history gives no details of his exploits on the battlefield. The one thing known for certain is that Pepin was finally victorious and that his victory was won just in time, for in the final months of the campaign he had become very ill, developing dropsy. When peace was concluded he started out for home without delay.

Due to his condition he found the journey long and exhausting. Reaching the Abbey of St. Denis, where he had been crowned by the Pope, he died on the twenty-fourth of September, 768.

Pepin was buried at St. Denis close to his father, Charles the Hammer. And according to his wishes and the custom of the time his realm was divided between his two sons. Countries and governments as we know them today did not exist at that time in Europe; they were only beginning to evolve. So Pepin divided his realm between his sons as though it were his private property.

Two weeks after their father's burial, the two brothers were hailed as kings at identical coronation ceremonies on the very same day. Before a great gathering of people and amid the clash of spears and resounding cries of "May the king live forever," Charles was raised upon the shields of his nobles at Noyons, in what is today northern France, while Carloman was being hailed and raised upon the shields of his nobles at the town of Soissons only a few miles to the south.

Charles, who was twenty-six, and Carloman, who was only sixteen, now each had a kingdom of his own. But Pepin, their late father, having assumed that they loved each other, left instructions that they were to rule the divided realm as though it were still one kingdom!

2

The Divided Kingdom

Young King Charles was intelligent, tall and handsome.
Einhard, who grew up in his court and later served as his
architect and secretary, has left us a full picture.

In his *The Life of Charlemagne*, the first biography of a
medieval king, Einhard describes Charles in the following
words:

> Charles was large and strong and of lofty stature
> though not too tall; his height was seven times the

length of his foot [six feet four inches]. The top of his head was round, his eyes very large and keen, his nose large and longer than average, his hair blond and his face pleasant and cheerful. His appearance was always stately and dignified whether he was standing or sitting, although his neck was thick and somewhat short . . . but the symmetry of the rest of his body concealed these defects. His stride was firm, his whole carriage manly, and his voice clear, but not so strong as his size led one to expect. His health was excellent.

Charles was temperate in eating and drinking. "He abominated drunkenness in anybody." His favorite food was roasted meat, "which his huntsmen used to bring in on the spit."

Charles also had plain tastes in dress. He always wore his simple national Frankish costume. "He despised foreign costumes however handsome and never allowed himself to be robed in them" except twice later in his life, in Rome, to please the Pope. "On great feastdays he made use of embroidered clothes and shoes bedecked with precious stones . . . and he appeared crowned with a diadem of gold and gems, but on other days his dress varied little from the common dress of the people."

Swimming was one of Charles' favorite sports. He was also an excellent horseman and had a passion for hunting. His daring and strength while on the hunt were such that legends arose about him. People and minstrels throughout the land sang his praises and told how he pursued the swift stag, braved the enraged boar and hunted the wild bull singlehanded.

The fame of his strength was such that they said he could fell a horse and rider with one blow of his fist, straighten out four horseshoes grasped together and lift a fully equipped soldier to the level of his head with his right hand alone.

But young King Charles was not all bravery and brawn. He was a well-educated man for his day. His father had maintained a school at the palace for his two sons and the other children of the court. There, vestiges of classical learning were taught, and there Charles received what instruction was available in the seven liberal arts: grammar, logic, rhetoric, arithmetic, music, astronomy and geometry. He was very good at arithmetic. He was also greatly interested in astronomy and music. And although we do not know if he ever played a musical instrument, it is recorded that there was an organ at one of his father's many palaces. The emperor in Constantinople had sent it as a gift to King Pepin. It was the first organ in Frankland and was the wonder and marvel of all who heard it.

Charles also showed a marked interest in grammar and rhetoric. He was an excellent speaker and linguist. Einhard says, "Charles had the gift of ready and fluent speech and could express whatever he had to say with the utmost clearness. He was not satisfied with the command of his native language only but also studied foreign ones and was such a master of Latin that he could speak it as fluently as his native tongue." He liked to use the Latin form of his name Carolus. He also understood Greek, although he spoke it with difficulty.

Charles was an eager student, and his early education went far beyond the seven liberal arts because he very fortunately came under the influence of the learned Abbé Fulrad of St. Denis, one of his father's most trusted advisers. This wise man instructed him not only in the tenets of the Catholic faith but also in the fine art of statecraft, the knowledge of which was to prove invaluable to Charles in his role as King of the Franks.

Young Charles and the Abbé Fulrad were devoted to each other. But when Pepin died and the kingdom was divided, they were separated, as St. Denis fell into that half of the Frankish realm deeded to Charles' young brother Carloman. However, the separation proved to be a short one because of a series of events which occurred with great rapidity and which nullified the dead King Pepin's wishes.

Shortly after Charles and Carloman inherited their kingdoms, open hostility broke out between them. Carloman, who was only sixteen, ten years younger than Charles, fell under the influence of evil men. These nobles poisoned him against Charles and led him to believe that he was the sole and rightful heir to his father's kingdom. They proposed ways in which he might eliminate Charles.

Luckily for Charles these crafty schemes were interrupted by a revolt in Aquitaine, which was in Carloman's domain. Following his father's wish that his two sons should rule as one, Charles immediately marched his army into Aquitaine, planning to join forces with Carloman's army. But Carloman had other ideas and refused to help. So Charles had to put down the revolt alone.

Since Aquitaine was a battleground and its people an enemy which Charles knew well, having fought there under his father for nine long years, he was able to bring Aquitaine to its knees in two short months. His military victory was swift indeed, and had Charles followed the pattern of most victorious generals he would have left an army of occupation in Aquitaine and returned home to wait until the next revolt occurred. But Charles, having been carefully trained in statecraft by the Abbé Fulrad, tried a new and different method based on ancient Germanic custom.

Believing that lasting peace and loyalty could only be won through tolerance, justice and understanding, he withdrew his army and issued a "capitulary," or list of written laws and regulations, for the governing and well-being of the people he had just conquered. This capitulary, while clearly stating that the Aquitainians must recognize the Franks as their lords and assist them in war, allowed the Aquitainians to rule themselves according to their ancient laws and traditions. They were to be a state within a state.

Charles' judgment proved correct. Aquitaine never again found cause to revolt. It became an integral part of the Frankish state. Pleased with the results of this, his first capitulary, Charles used it as a pattern for all his future conquests. The wisdom and tolerance he displayed in this regard accounts for his tremendous success as a conqueror and ruler.

Charles was extremely satisfied with his success in Aquitaine, but he was deeply troubled by his brother's hostility. He was wise enough to realize that he must act decisively and at once in order to protect himself. And so he decided to try to make friends and allies of the King of the Lombards and the Duke of Bavaria and thereby isolate Carloman.

Although he was married to a "noble Frankish lady" named Himiltrude, whom his father had given him as a bride some years before, and although she had borne him two children whom he adored, a little hunchback son named Pepin and a daughter, Rothaid, he decided to leave her and marry again. His choice was one of the three daughters of the King of the Lombards, whom Pepin the Short had conquered only a few years before! Her name was Desiderata, and her sister, the Princess Liutperga, was wife to the Duke of Bavaria. Thus, with one stroke Charles planned to embrace both families and win their undying friendship!

To gain this end Charles was even willing to overlook the fact that Tassilo, the Duke of Bavaria, who was his cousin, had broken the most solemn vows of vassal to lord. Bavaria had once belonged to Frankland, but while his father, Pepin, was waging his nine-year war against Aquitaine, Tassilo had declared Bavaria independent. He had repudiated the oath of allegiance he had once sworn to King Pepin, Charles and Carloman upon the most sacred "bones of St. Denis, St. Germain and St. Martin."

THE DIVIDED KINGDOM

Queen Bertrada, who seems to have sided with Charles in his difficulties with Carloman, went to Italy to negotiate with the King of the Lombards. It was not an easy matter for her to overcome the hostility of the King of the Lombards against the Frankish royal family, but since she was an intelligent and forceful woman, she returned a few weeks later bringing Desiderata with her.

Everyone was pleased with the political alliance which had thus been secured, everyone that is except Carloman and the new pope, Stephen III.

Pope Stephen was against this marriage for two reasons: Charles was already married, and the Lombards whose lands surrounded the Papal State and Rome were his deadly enemies. He wrote King Charles a letter using the plainest language.

> Would it not be the height of madness if the glorious race of the Franks and your own noble royal dynasty were to be contaminated by a union with the faithless and stinking Lombards, who cannot even be called a nation and who have brought leprosy into the world? . . . By the will of God and your father's choice you are already united in lawful marriage with a beautiful wife of your own Frankish race. . . . How can you make common cause with those treacherous Lombards who are always in arms against the Church of God and who have invaded our province of Rome?

The Pope's letter closed with a terrifying threat:

CHARLEMAGNE

Saint Peter himself, prince of the apostles, guardian of the keys to the Kingdom of Heaven . . . commands you not to wed the daughter of the Lombard king . . . Should you do what is unpleasing to God and have the temerity to ignore our protests, be warned that by the authority of St. Peter you are then under the most fearful curse, an outcast from the kingdom of God and doomed with the devil and his most wicked assistants and all impious men to the eternal flames.

Charles was a very religious person and attended mass every morning, but the Pope's letter did not frighten him. While the Pope considered himself above all earthly kings, Charles held a different opinion. He felt that the Pope was only head of the Church in Rome, and as a king he had no intentions of taking orders from him. Therefore, disregarding the flames of hell he went ahead with his plans and married Desiderata.

Charles' plan for winning allies by a political marriage appeared to be a wise one. However, it failed and because of a very simple reason. Charles did not like the Lombard princess, and in less than a year and with a rashness which was quite foreign to him, he divorced her, sent her back to her father and married a beautiful Swabian girl of noble birth called Hildegarde. Charles was twenty-nine years old and Hildegarde was only twelve or thirteen.

Queen Bertrada was infuriated at her son's behavior. She did not mind his marrying such a young girl, because many girls married as young in those days; she was angry because he had acted against her wishes and because of the political complications which his act was certain to bring about. Many of his friends, counselors, relatives and nobles were also disturbed at this insult to the King of the Lombards. A few actually withdrew their allegiance from Charles and left his domain.

However, Charles was not disturbed and Hildegarde proved to be a good wife. In the years that followed she bore him four sons and five daughters, all of whom he adored. She took loving care of his son Pepin the Hunchback and his daughter Rothaid, just as though they were her own children. And being gentle and affectionate, she created a home that was filled with happiness.

The King of the Lombards and his whole family were naturally enraged by the insult they had suffered at the hands of Charles. So Charles, who had plotted to isolate Carloman, now found himself isolated instead. To the south there were his treacherous brother and Lombardy. To the east were the Bavarians. Should these enemies join forces against him, he would be overwhelmed.

But fortune was on the side of Charles. Just at this critical moment, his brother Carloman was taken seriously ill. Feeling that his brother's chances of survival were small, and to thwart any plan to place Carloman's two little sons upon the throne, Charles massed his army in readiness on the border of Carloman's realm.

A few days later, on December 4, 771, when Carloman

died, Charles marched boldly forward. He crossed the border and pushed deep into his brother's territory. Then calling an assembly of the great nobles of his brother's domain, he asked them to accept him as king.

The Abbé Fulrad, his beloved friend and teacher, was the first to swear allegiance to Charles. He was followed by most of the other lords of the land, who saw the wisdom of having a united kingdom and who had been impressed by the daring and decisiveness of the young man. Only a handful of nobles refused. They fled with the widowed queen and her two little sons to Lombardy, where they hoped to persuade the King of the Lombards to declare war upon Charles.

So it came to pass that in three years time, the Frankish kingdom, which Pepin the Short had divided between his two sons as though it were a private estate, was once more welded into a great realm.

3

The Road to Conquest

With the Frankish kingdom once more united, Charles became the most powerful ruler in Europe. Overnight, by a miraculous stroke of fortune, his kingdom had been doubled in size and his enemies had been rendered helpless.

The King of the Lombards and Tassilo of Bavaria did not dare to attack him. Even though Carloman's widow and the nobles who had fled with her did all they could to provoke the King of the Lombards into action against

Charles, he could not be persuaded. Instead he returned to his old and favorite pursuit of attacking his helpless neighbor the pope, and capturing lands and cities claimed by the Papacy.

Stephen III had died and a Roman aristocrat, a very able, intelligent and courageous man, had been elected pope, taking the name of Hadrian I. This new pope refused to be intimidated by the King of the Lombards' demands that he return the cities and lands he had taken, and Hadrian expelled from the Vatican all those with pro-Lombard sympathies, including even the papal chancellor. When the King of the Lombards led his army against Rome, the Pope defied them boldly with his spiritual authority. He threatened the entire army with excommunication and eternal damnation. The King of the Lombards was unmoved by this threat, but the rank and file were filled with fear and refused to fight.

Rome had been saved—temporarily. Hadrian knew there would be other attacks, and he feared that next time he would not be so successful. So he sent emissaries with all haste to Charles, the Patriarch of Rome, begging for help.

Charles, however, did not respond. He had little sympathy for the Vatican's claims, even though they were now largely based on Pepin's "Donation." Besides, he had no intention of taking orders from the Pope. He wanted the Pope to understand that the King of the Franks was his master and that the Frankish army was not at his disposal. He decided to let the Pope wait while he occupied himself with a matter he found much more interesting, a campaign against the Saxons, those barbaric pagan people living in the dark forests north and east of the Rhine. For some years the Saxons had been attacking missionaries, raiding his borders, burning churches and terrorizing his people; and Charles had decided that the time had come to teach these godless people a lesson.

The Saxons loved their pagan gods such as Woden, Thor the Thunderer, Freya the goddess of fruitfulness and love, and Hela the goddess of the underworld. They were devoted to the deities they believed inhabited every spring, rock and oak and to the vampires and werewolves they thought roamed the forests. They hated the people of the Frankish kingdom who were Christians and who were constantly sending missionaries into their land to convert them and build churches.

The Saxons hated these Christians who insisted that they give up the gods whom they had worshiped since the dawn of time and cast aside their belief in omens and amulets. How could they be safe until a sacred furrow had been plowed around their homestead? How could their harvest be spared from hail and blight if they did not offer feasts and processions to the earth gods? What comfort could Christianity offer if these were removed? They did not like the idea of the Christian god who was so strict and who would punish one for the slightest misstep. They did not like giving up meat during Lent and being limited to only one wife.

Besides they had not forgotten how Boniface, the aged Benedictine monk from England who had crowned King Pepin the Short, had come into their lands as an envoy of the pope and had boldly taken an axe and chopped down the great oak in Hesse which was sacred to Thor.

Yes, the Saxons had many grievances against the people of the Frankish kingdom because of Christianity. Besides they were a warlike people. They loved to sit around a campfire at night or in the great log halls of their chieftains drinking beer and boasting of their exploits. In the morning, intoxicated by both the beer and the boasting, it was natural for them to form into bands and raid the Frankish settlements on the border, devastating the crops and burning down the churches.

These Saxon raids along the Frankish border were not a serious threat to Frankland. But Charles, who in spite of his attitude toward the Pope was a very religious Christian, decided to put an end to them and bring the taming influence of Christianity to these warlike and neglected children of God. He truly felt that it was his duty as a Christian king to defend the Church from all enemies and spread the teachings of Christ. At the Field of March, which was held that spring at Worms just south of Saxony, he laid bare his plan. His nobles and chiefs who enjoyed war and the prospect of booty readily gave their consent. They went back to their homelands and began mobilizing their people, informing them as to the enemy and the place where the host was to convene.

Every landholder was expected to serve under the banner of his count; military service was each Frank's obligation to his king. Poor men came on foot armed with lance, wooden shield, bow and twelve arrows. From the wide leather belt, which all Franks wore to gather their tunics, hung an axe, a knife and such toilet articles as rude scissors and a comb made of wood or bone. Those who were too poor for such weapons and tools were required to appear armed with knotted clubs, scythes and flails. They sometimes also carried shields which they had woven from supple twigs. The rich, who rode on horseback, wore shirts of mail, iron helmets and carried a sword and dagger besides a lance, bow and arrows and wooden shield covered with leather and ornamented with an elaborately etched metal disk in its center.

Each local contingent was also required to bring along a number of wagons covered with leather and containing food for three months, arms and clothing for six months and tools for the digging of trenches and for the building of ladders and other equipment needed during a siege.

The gathering of the Frankish host was both a strange and glorious sight. Colorful banners fluttered in the breeze. Armor and lances glistened in the sun. Clouds of dust rose as thousands of feet and horses hoofs beat the earth. The voices and shouts of men, the neighing of horses, the lowing of oxen and the clear sound of trumpets mingled in a symphony of sound. At night the darkness was studded with campfires around which the men gathered to sing songs and tell tales of brave deeds.

As each new contingent arrived, those on horseback were separated from those on foot. Mounted men formed the cavalry, whose duty it was to lead the attacks. Those on foot formed the infantry, whose task it was to finish off the foe and mop up after the cavalry charge. Behind these two fighting forces and at a good distance would come the long train of ox-drawn supply carts.

This was the sight which presented itself each time the host gathered, and so it was that spring when Charles assembled his army for his first campaign after becoming sole King of the Franks. As soon as everything was ready, he marched into the land of the Saxons heading directly for the center of their religious life in the heart of their territory. There in a sacred grove stood an ancient tree which they called the Irminsul and which represented the mythical tree which they believed supported the universe. Around the Irminsul was a ring of log halls that served as dwellings for the priests and in which was stored a great treasure of gold and silver that through the centuries the Saxons had brought as offerings to their gods.

Charles and his army moved with such speed that the Saxons, who did not have an organized army and did not understand cavalry charges and infantry attacks, preferring swift raids, were taken by surprise. They did not have time to gather their forces and defend their sacred grove.

Following the example set by Boniface many years before, Charles cut down the sacred Irminsul. He then ordered his soldiers to destroy the ring of buildings, a task which took three full days. The gold and silver treasure he divided among his men.

Charles now led his army deeper into Saxony, laying waste the settlements and countryside as he advanced. He encountered little or no resistance. Reaching the Weser River he was met by emissaries from several different Saxon tribes asking for peace.

Charles, who was an unusually kind and tolerant conqueror and ruler for those times, felt that he had accomplished his purpose. He thought that the Saxons had now learned their lesson and would never again raid Frankish territory, burn down churches and terrorize Christian missionaries. He was willing to make peace and, in fact, made a very generous one. He asked for only twelve hostages as proof of Saxon goodwill, and withdrew his forces!

By the middle of October he was back in his palace at Heristal just south of the Rhine, where his beloved young Hildegarde awaited him with her firstborn child, an infant only a few days old. It was a boy and he was named Charles after his father the king and his great-grandfather, Charles the Hammer.

As soon as Hildegarde and the infant could travel, Charles moved his family and court to his palace at Thionville on the Moselle about a hundred miles to the southeast. He hoped to spend some weeks there hunting with his friends, but he had no sooner settled down at this royal estate than envoys arrived from both Pope Hadrian and the King of the Lombards, asking him to mediate the differences which existed between them.

Charles was flattered that these two high personages should appeal to him instead of to the Emperor in Constantinople. It indicated the respect in which he was held. Although he still had little sympathy for the Pope's claims, he felt it was his duty to honor his father's "Donation" to the Papacy. Trying to avoid war, he offered the King of the Lombards a huge sum of gold, fourteen thousand large gold coins, if he would surrender all claims to the disputed lands and cities. The King of the Lombards would not accept this offer.

Charles was forced to bring the matter to the general assembly or the Field of March which was held in May to make it easier for those who had to come from distant parts. The general assembly was reluctant to allow him to declare war against the Lombards in support of the Papacy. They were suspicious of the Pope's claims and irritated by his constant complaints. However, at Charles' insistence, they finally agreed to raise the necessary forces, and Geneva was chosen as the place where the host should gather.

When all was ready Charles divided his army into two parts. He placed one section under the command of his uncle Bernard and sent it over the eight-thousand-foot Alpine pass of Mount Jupiter, later known as the Great St. Bernard Pass. The other section under the command of

Charles himself went through the pass of Mount Cenis about fifty miles to the west.

The King of the Lombards, feeling certain that Charles would use this pass, had built fortifications at its narrow exit and was waiting for him there with his entire army. Still hoping to avoid war Charles once more offered his former father-in-law gold for the return of the disputed lands and cities. But the King of the Lombards, ignorant of the fact that another Frankish army was at that very moment coming through the Jupiter Pass, again refused Charles' offer.

These negotiations had taken time, and time was on the side of Charles. When the King of the Lombards reached his decision, the second Frankish army was in sight. Overwhelmed, the King of the Lombards and his troops fled to the south. He took refuge behind the stout walls of his capital, the city of Pavia, while his son, Adelchis, sought the safety of Verona.

Drawing up before the walls of Pavia, Charles at once saw that the city could be taken only after a long siege. It would have to be starved out, and so he decided to settle down and make himself comfortable.

To seal the city off from all supplies he ringed it with troops, a deep trench and a series of fortifications. Then for his comfort and the comfort of those nobles and churchmen who had come with him from Frankland, he ordered a chapel and a whole village of huts constructed. And he sent for Hildegarde.

She was expecting her second child, but being a dutiful

and loving wife she made the long hard journey. Riding on horseback and bringing the baby Charles with her, she crossed the Alps into Lombardy. There a few months later, beside the walls of the besieged city of Pavia, she gave birth to a little girl, whom she and Charles named Adalhaid.

Charles spent Christmas with Hildegarde and his children at Pavia. Then leaving the siege in charge of his capable uncle Bernard, he took a small detachment of troops and marched eastward across Italy to Verona.

He wanted to capture Adelchis, the son of the King of the Lombards, but Adelchis was no longer there. He had fled Lombardy and was on his way to Constantinople, where he hoped to win the Emperor's support against Charles. Verona surrendered without giving battle, and the only captives Charles took were his brother Carloman's widow, her two little sons and the Frankish nobles who had fled with her. They came out of the city gate and, falling to their knees, pleaded for mercy.

This was hardly necessary, for Charles was seldom vindictive; although he could on occasion be roused to violent anger, he was usually gentle and tolerant. He forgave the nobles and invited them back to Frankland. History leaves no record of what became of Carloman's widow and sons, but it is probable that to prevent any future claims on his kingdom, Charles persuaded the mother to become a nun and had the boys entered in an order of monks.

This was the humane method Charles used for disposing of his enemies, in those days when torture, blinding, maiming and death were the punishments usually meted out by conquerors.

Charles was very pleased with the way his campaign in Lombardy had gone. Verona had fallen and he knew that Pavia would, in a short time, also surrender. Besides, the people of Lombardy, who were Germanic in origin like the Franks, seemed to accept him. They were surprisingly friendly. They did not seem to care who ruled over them, their own king or the king of the Franks.

The campaign was really over. Only one trouble confronted Charles, and that involved the Pope. Reports had reached Charles that while he was occupied fighting the Lombards in northern Italy, the Pope had seized the Lombard territories east and south of Rome. He had taken the Duchy of Beneventum and the Duchy of Spoletum and incorporated them into his Papal State.

Hadrian had done this in secret without consulting Charles, and when he heard about it he was greatly disturbed. He felt that the Pope was defying his authority and was trying to place himself above him. So he decided to go to Rome and talk to Hadrian. He had never been to Rome and spring was at hand; he wanted to celebrate Easter in the Holy City.

4

Easter in Rome

Charles started out for Rome at the head of a great procession. He was accompanied by Hildegarde and the two babies and their nurses and attendants as well as a large body made up of every bishop, abbot, priest and noble who had come with him and his army into Lombardy. All, in fact, who were not directly occupied with the siege of Pavia joined the king. Everyone was eager, for in those days it was the hope and dream of every Christian to make at least one pilgrimage during his lifetime to Rome, the wellspring

44

of his faith, to visit the many holy shrines and do penance for his sins.

The great and joyous procession, guarded by soldiers, started out from Pavia at the end of March and wended its way slowly southward toward the Eternal City. It was a long journey of some 275 miles, and while there were still good Roman roads in those parts, it was nonetheless difficult. Streams and rivers had to be crossed as well as the rugged Apennines. And each night camp had to be made out under the open skies.

Slowly the procession advanced, and all who saw it pass clearly guessed its destination; yet Pope Hadrian did not learn of its existence until it was already close to the city. Charles was so irritated with the Pope that he had not informed His Holiness of his intended visit, and the Pope sensing his anger was deeply distressed. Nevertheless, he made hurried and elaborate plans for receiving Charles, King of the Franks and Patriarch of Rome, and proclaiming him as the deliverer of Rome.

Officials of Rome, tribunes and consuls, men who still bore titles from the ancient days of the Caesars, awaited the arrival of Charles thirty miles from the city walls. There they presented him with the banner of the Militia of Rome, the equivalent of the keys to the city.

At a distance of one mile from the city walls, Charles was hailed by the militia. There were also bands of children waving branches of palm and olive and singing hymns and songs of praise.

Next came the Roman clergy carrying crosses and the banners of the saints. Seeing them Charles dismounted, and with banners waving and the air filled with song, he made his way on foot to St. Peter's, a massive church with a great wooden roof which stood unprotected outside the city walls. It had been built during the fourth century over Peter's burial place and close to Nero's Circus where Peter, the first Bishop of Rome, had been crucified head downward by the Romans.

Pope Hadrian, together with the highest Church dignitaries, had been awaiting the arrival of Charles since dawn. Now he stood at the top of the steps of St. Peter's ready to greet the Frankish king. But Charles, filled with reverence for Peter, kept him waiting. He knelt and kissed each step as he ascended.

Reaching the top, Charles embraced the Pope as a friend but not as his equal. To indicate clearly to all present that he, Charles, King of the Franks, was the Pope's superior, he took his position at Hadrian's right hand. Retaining this position, he then walked with the Pope through the great bronze doors and into the basilica where a vast throng of clergy greeted him with the words, "Blessed be he who comes in the name of the Lord!"

Advancing slowly to the tomb of Peter, Charles fell to his knees and bowed his head in most reverent prayer.

The following day was Easter Sunday, and after attending mass, Charles visited many of the churches with which the city abounded and prayed before the relics for which they were famous.

On the days that followed he visited other places of interest in Rome, the remains and ruins of a great empire, which in that spring of 774 was no longer the glorious city of the Caesars. Two centuries of barbarian invasions and occupation had reduced Rome to a pitiful state.

Rome had been sacked three times during the fifth century and besieged five times during the sixth century. Its wondrous aqueducts had been destroyed, and the people had been forced to drink the waters of the Tiber. The broken aqueducts disgorged their waters in the country around Rome forming great swamps which were the breeding places for malaria and other pestilence. The population which had once numbered more than a million had sunk to fifty thousand. Many of the rich and noble had moved to the new capital, Constantinople, abandoning their palaces.

With the decay of the city and the decline of the population civic pride had diminished. Marble statues of great beauty had been broken up and thrown into the lime kilns. Temples and palaces had been stripped of their marble facings to supply material for the building of churches and paving of roads. Marble bathtubs were now used as baptismal fonts, and marble chairs, which had once been used by Roman senators, served as thrones for bishops and other Church dignitaries.

As Charles and his friends wandered about they saw many

abandoned palaces, deserted pagan temples, unused amphi-theaters and public baths. However, while grass grew in many streets there were two places Charles must have visited which still seethed with excitement as in the past: games were still held in the Coliseum, and the Forum, the very heart of the ancient Roman Empire, still pulsed with life.

While Charles spent many pleasant days admiring the beauties and wonders of Rome, he did not forget the main purpose of his visit. He held several meetings with Pope Hadrian to discuss the question of the Duchies of Beneven-tum and Spoletum.

The Pope was frank in stating why he had taken these two duchies. He said that it was his plan to capture enough ter-ritory around Rome to enable the Papacy to exist as an independent state—a country large enough and populous enough to defend itself against all aggression.

Charles was not pleased to hear of the Pope's plan. He wanted to keep the Papacy as a purely spiritual force under his domination. He refused to recognize the Pope's an-nexation of Beneventum and Spoletum, insisting that he, Charles, was sole master of all Lombard territory in Italy. However, he offered Hadrian balm for his wounds. He vowed that he would not rest until all Europe was Chris-tianized—this was not much of a concession for he had al-ready started Christianizing pagan Saxony, believing it was his duty to do so as a Christian and a king. And he offered to reaffirm Pepin's "Donation."

We do not know whether Hadrian was taken in by

Charles' promises or whether, being a man of wisdom, he knew when he was defeated. At any rate he gave up the two coveted duchies and accepted Charles' plan instead. A few days later, in a solemn ceremony in St. Peter's, Charles presented Hadrian with a new copy of his father's gift, placing it beneath the copies of the Gospel which rested on St. Peter's tomb.

No promise could have been more sacred. Yet in the years that followed, Charles and Hadrian were constantly at odds as to the extent of the lands and the authority granted in the document, all copies of which have unfortunately been destroyed, so that no one knows who was correct. While Charles claimed dominion over all Lombard territory in Italy, the Pope claimed that Pepin's Donation granted him almost all of Italy including Venice, Istria and the Island of Corsica, territories over which Charles and his father never had any authority!

Having settled his problems with the Pope, Charles now returned to the siege of Pavia. Weakened by starvation and disease its people were no longer able to hold out. A few weeks after his return, at the end of nine full months of siege, the city surrendered.

The King of the Lombards, his wife and a daughter, who was probably Desiderata, Charles' ex-wife, came out through the city gates and threw themselves upon the mercy of the King of the Franks. Charles was merciful, and as was his custom, he had the King of the Lombards enrolled as a monk in a monastery deep in the heart of Frankland. The Queen and her daughter were forced to take vows and enter a nunnery.

With the fall of Pavia, Lombardy's two hundred years of independent rule came to an end. It now belonged to Charles. But he did not subject it to the brutalities which most conquerors imposed on the vanquished in those days. He instituted "self-rule" in Lombardy as he had in Aquitaine some time before. Appointing Lombards who were friendly to him to all key positions, he allowed the Lombards to rule themselves according to their ancient laws and customs. Of course, all Lombard noblemen had to swear allegiance to him. They had to kneel before him and, placing their hands in his, recite this solemn oath: "Great and powerful king, God has given the world to you for the good of mankind, and I shall honor and serve you faithfully for all time."

Henceforth Lombards would serve in his army, increasing its size and strength. Lombardy's enormous treasury of gold and silver was also his. And he could look forward to a large yearly revenue from this land which traded with Constantinople and the rich East and which taxed all goods and produce which were imported or exported.

Lombardy was a rich prize indeed, and Charles, who had come rather unwillingly to Italy to help the Pope and save Rome, was very pleased. He was thirty-two years old, and it was only six years since he had mounted the throne. In that short time he had more than doubled his kingdom. Following his brother Carloman's death he had annexed all of his lands; he had then subdued the Saxons and had now added the whole of the kingdom of Lombardy to his realm. Henceforth he called himself Charles, King of the Franks and King of the Lombards.

Only one shadow darkened his happiness. Fearing that the intense heat of the Italian summer would be dangerous for his little daughter Adalhaid, he had sent her north with her nurse and attendants. However, the trip had proved too much and the infant had died.

5

Life in Frankland

Charles spent the winter of 774–775 in Frankland attending to the various problems which had arisen during his absence. There were many royal estates scattered throughout the land, and according to Frankish custom Charles, together with his wife and children and the entire court, visited one after the other, completing a circuit of the realm each year. Frankland had no capital, and journeying from one royal estate to another brought the King into direct contact with the many different peoples of his kingdom and their special problems.

Charles' royal residences did not in any way resemble the great stone feudal castles of the later Middle Ages. Those in the Rhine Valley and other northern districts were rather crude and rustic. They were for the most part made of roughly hewn timbers and consisted of a large banqueting hall on the first floor with family rooms above. The only distinctive feature was a portico or porch running on all four sides and decorated with carving and painting.

His residences in the south, especially in Aquitaine and Lombardy, were very different from those in the north. They were truly luxurious by comparison, built in the Roman manner. The rooms—throne room, a great hall for dining, family rooms and kitchen—were built around a central court. There were baths. There were hot and cold running water and an ingenious system of heating the rooms by circulating hot water or hot air through a system of pipes.

The architecture varied from north to south but the general layout of the surrounding grounds was the same. Close by the palace were the rude huts of the peasants who farmed the royal estate, barns for the cattle, stables for horses, sheepfolds and pigsties. There were also granaries, a mill, a blacksmith shop, sheds where wine was made and beer brewed, a dairy where butter and cheese were produced and buildings where the queen supervised the spinning of flax and wool, the weaving of cloth and the making of tapestries and clothes.

CHARLEMAGNE

Each royal estate was under the care of a steward from whom Charles demanded a detailed yearly report. Very fortunately one of these reports has survived. Among other things it lists all the produce raised on the estate. There were wheat, rye, oats, barley, beans and peas. Because of the great amount of beer consumed there was fifteen times as much barley planted as rye or wheat. The inventory of livestock lists: "51 head of old cattle, 5 three-year olds, 7 two-year olds, 7 yearlings, horses, 50 cows, 20 young bulls, 38 yearling calves, 3 old bulls, 260 hogs, 100 young pigs, 5 boars, 150 sheep, 200 lambs, 120 rams, 30 goats, 3 bucks, 30 geese, 80 chickens and 22 peacocks."

Some of Charles' decrees concerning the running of his estates, or *vills*, as they were called, have also survived. From them we learn that he was very particular and very advanced for his day. He would not tolerate any poaching in his royal forests and gave strict orders that all wolves must be destroyed. If fish was taken from his streams and ponds to be sold in the market, the streams and ponds had to be restocked. Each estate must provide "blankets, pillows, bedclothes and coverings for tables and benches" so that he and his court would no longer have to be inconvenienced by carrying these from palace to palace. Buildings must be repaired promptly and not allowed to fall into ruin. And he insisted on "the greatest cleanliness" in the handling of meat and dairy products and in the making of wine. He would not allow the treading of grapes with bare feet in any of his wineries.

Charles also showed a keen interest in beekeeping, and he named the many plants and trees he wanted grown in his vegetable gardens and orchards. Among the plants there were to be lettuce, peas, beans, cabbage, carrots, leeks, mint, savory, sage, tansy, strawberries, peaches, apples, pears, apricots and cherries. There were also to be flower beds and "swans, peacocks, pheasants, ducks, pigeons, partridges and turtledoves for the sake of ornament."

All these things Charles ordered. He was interested in everything that pertained to his estates. No detail was so trifling as to escape his attention.

It was a happy time when Charles and his court traveled through the realm. It was a time for seeing old friends and making new ones. It was a time for exchanging news and gossip. Although Charles was a moderate person and did not approve of excessive eating and drinking, it was a time for feasts and banquets and rousing hunts through the royal forests. He loved nothing better than hunting, and dressed in his simple Frankish clothes he could ride or run through the thickest woods. But his nobles, especially those in Aquitaine, liked to wear costly silks, furs and feathers, which, much to his amusement, were soon torn to shreds.

However, while Charles entertained lavishly at each palace which he visited, he never forgot the main reason for his coming—the people. He was a serious and conscientious ruler and therefore spent many hours each day attending to his kingly duties. The days were, in fact, sometimes not long enough, and his secretary and biographer

Einhard tells us that in the morning, "While he was dressing and putting on his shoes, he not only gave audience to his friends but if the Count of the Palace told him of any suit on which his judgment was necessary, he had the parties brought before him forthwith, took cognizance of the case, and gave his decision, just as if he were sitting on the judgment seat."

According to the custom of the Franks and Charles' policy, the different peoples of the realm were ruled and judged by their traditional laws: the Burgundians lived and were judged under their laws, the Alemannians under their laws, the Lombards and Aquitainians under theirs. But if anyone had a complaint he had the right to appeal directly to the king. Charles had a knowledge of all the laws of all the people who lived in his realm. And regardless of the weight of the conflict, whether it was serious or only trifling, regardless of that person's position, Charles gave each case his most earnest attention.

Other problems which received Charles' attention during these visits were matters concerning the Church and the building of roads and bridges. Charles considered himself as head of the Church in his realm, and so he settled disputes between churchmen and personally investigated to see that the holy services were properly performed. He would drop in unexpectedly at baptisms and other services, and if any mistakes where made in the ceremony, he would reprimand the guilty priest and order that he return to his studies until he had properly learned his lessons. He also insisted that only classical Latin be used during services; he deplored the use by the priests of corrupt or vulgarized Latin, which was mixed with local dialects.

Traveling through his realm as Charles did he was very aware of the lack of roads. The only roads that existed were those which the Romans had built centuries before, and they were now in deplorable condition. During the early years of his reign, he launched a road-building program. He required each district to build roads, and he instituted a law, the principle of which survives to this day, that the people owning the land along the road were responsible for its maintenance.

Charles also inaugurated a program of bridge building. Anyone who built a proper bridge across a stream or river was permitted to charge a toll. However, the owner of the bridge could not force people to cross his bridge if they preferred to ford the stream or use a raft or boat.

The people of Charles' realm were divided into three main classes: churchmen, nobles and peasants.

The Church held great tracts of land which had been presented to it by penitent kings, nobles and peasants. It has been estimated that at different periods during the Middle Ages the Church owned as much as one-third of all the land in Europe. While some priests and monks lived simple lives tending to a village church, the vast majority of bishops, priests, abbots and monks lived on great estates similar to those belonging to the king. The monks did most of the work, serving as masons, carpenters, sculptors, bakers, brewers, and tending the cattle and tilling the soil. But some of the Church estates were so vast that large tracts of the land were lent out to peasants who tilled them as their own, sharing the produce with the monastery.

The nobles of Charles' realm also owned great estates managed by stewards and worked by serfs and freemen. Slavery was almost nonexistent because, from its earliest beginnings, the Church had outlawed slavery among Christians. One Christian could not hold another Christian in slavery; he could only have pagan or non-Christian slaves. And since it was further every Christian's duty to try to convert pagans and other non-Christians, slavery, which had been so widespread under the Romans, had by this time almost completely disappeared in Europe.

Serfs were freemen who had given up their freedom and the freedom of their future heirs and bound themselves to a lord in return for a cottage to live in, a piece of land to till and protection from robbers, marauding bands and enemy invasions. Charles did not approve of men giving up their freedom and ruled against serfdom, thereby keeping it in check during his lifetime. Feudalism and serfdom, which were so characteristic of the Middle Ages, began to flourish only after his death.

Some peasants, a very few, were comfortably off owning a good cottage and enough land and livestock to provide them and their families with all they needed. However, most peasants, serf and freeman alike, lived in hopeless, abject poverty. The ordinary peasant's abode was nothing more than a hovel with a thatched roof and earthen floor. It consisted of one room which he and his family shared with whatever livestock he owned. He and his wife and children slept huddled together on a pile of hay or rags in one corner. If they were fortunate they had a crude table, bench, cooking pot, a few crude tools for tilling the soil, a pig, three or four hens and ducks. A man who owned a cow was looked upon as very successful.

The serf owed his lord part of everything he raised and several days work each week. He also had to give his lord's steward gifts of such precious things as eggs, wine, grain and suckling pigs. He dared not withhold these bribes. The freeman, who owned his own land, naturally kept all the fruits of his labor. However, whether a man was serf or free, he lived perpetually on the verge of starvation because the methods of agriculture were so primitive—there was at that time no knowledge of the benefits of fertilizer—that even good harvests were pitifully meager.

The peasant's life was hard beyond belief and his poverty appalling. Yet the Church, like the lord, also received a part of his labors, for everyone, rich and poor, serf and freeman, was required to pay a tithe or one-tenth of all the food he raised and of all the increase of poultry and livestock to the Church.

The people—king, churchmen, nobles and peasants, alike—were extremely superstitious. Christianity had not yet completely eradicated the many primitive and pagan beliefs of their barbaric ancestors. They believed in omens, dreams and the devil. They rang church bells to drive evil spirits away.

The peasants were the most superstitious of all. They were extremely ignorant and therefore lived in constant fear. If their cows, oxen or children were sick they recited ancient incantations and sometimes consulted magicians or wizards. They recited special charms when tending their swarming bees, stamping their grapes or gathering their harvest. In fact, they had charms for every task which they performed.

The Church disapproved of these remnants of paganism but was not able to erase them. And so it compromised. It asked that the people add the words "So be it, Lord" to the end of their incantations and that they appeal to the Virgin Mary instead of to Mother Earth. And it attributed magical powers to its saints. Each saint became a specialist. St. Corneille became the protector of oxen, St. Anthony of pigs and St. Gall of chickens. St. Sebastian took care of pestilence. St. Apollinia, whose jaw had been broken by his executioner, took care of toothache, and St. Roche of sore throat. And to check whether the people were obeying Church rules the Church required them to confess to their priests what they had done when their oxen or chickens were sick and whether or not they had recently consulted a magician.

The peasant's life was hard and filled with fear and uncertainty. But he also knew moments of pleasure and joy. There were feast days and fairs. Charles had decreed that on Sundays and saints' days no work could be done. So on saints' days they danced and drank and feasted in the church-yard with the priests joining in the fun.

On market days they brought their produce, sometimes only a chicken or a few eggs, to a nearby village or town. They would start out early in the morning and walk many miles. But it was worth it, for at the market they would meet other peasants who had come from other directions and they would exchange news and gossip.

However, the peasant's most exciting experience was to visit a big fair like the one held each year at St. Denis. There the peasant saw all sorts of wondrous things: silks, spices, perfumes and pearls brought from the Orient by merchants and peddlers. There were also products from distant parts of Europe, such as olive oil from Italy, wine from southern Gaul, amber from the Baltic, furs from the dark forest to the north and east, brass and iron utensils from Spain, brightly dyed woolen cloth from the Frisian Islands and woolen capes from what we know today as Flanders, capes so large and finely woven that they were already famous in Rome in Caesar's day.

Everything was for sale, and if one had a few coins or something to barter one could carry these treasures home. One might even be fortunate enough to buy a holy relic, for there were men at the fairs who had traveled to far-off Jerusalem and returned with such sacred treasures as water from the river Jordan, some of the original frankincense and myrrh which the Three Kings had brought from the East or threads from the gown of the Virgin.

CHARLEMAGNE

The excitement of the fair was further heightened by the many people who came from distant parts and wore strange costumes. There were men from England, Scotland and Ireland, princely merchants from Venice, bearded Jews from the Orient, Greeks and Syrians. There were also jugglers, minstrels, vendors of sweets and performing dogs and bear-baiting.

The wonder of it all was overwhelming. And the peasant returned home with enough to talk and dream about for a full year, at the end of which time there would surely be another great fair.

6

Widukind the Saxon

While Charles was traveling through his realm that winter of 774–775, he received distressing news concerning the Saxons. Those barbarian people to the north whom he had subdued before leaving on his conquest of Lombardy were again raiding his borders and burning churches.

Charles was angered by their behavior. Determined that he, as the King of the Franks, should serve as the champion of Christianity, he decided to wage a war against the pagan

Saxons until the very last of them was converted to Christianity—converted or annihilated.

Charles had a further reason for wanting to engage in an all-out war against the Saxons. These barbaric people had always lived in separate tribes choosing a national leader only in times of war, but now they were beginning to consolidate. A man named Widukind, one of their richest chiefs, a Westphalian related through marriage to the King of Denmark, was agitating for unity and winning great support among the common people.

So at the Field of March, which was held in July that year at Duren, not far from Aachen and only twenty miles from the Rhine, Charles presented his plan for an all-out war.

Winning the immediate support of the general assembly, Charles quickly gathered together his army and began his invasion. He crossed the Rhine so swiftly that the Saxons were again taken by surprise and unable to organize any defense. Within the first days the fortress of Sigiburg, a great Saxon stockade, fell after offering but little resistance.

Leaving a garrison at Sigiburg, Charles and his army now swept eastward through beautiful open farmlands to the fortress of Eresburg, which he had captured in his previous campaign and which the Saxons had recaptured and burned to the ground during his absence. Rebuilding this stockade and leaving it in control of a garrison, Charles plunged deep into Saxony, cutting a wide ribbon of devastation, trampling down the grain, burning settlements and slaughtering cattle.

WIDUKIND THE SAXON

He met no resistance until he had gone a hundred miles and reached the banks of the Weser River. There he was confronted by a small force of Saxons under a chief called Hessi; their lands lay to the east of the river.

Charles quickly overcame this show of resistance. Hessi and his people submitted, giving hostages and promising to embrace Christianity. Seeing this, their neighbors to the west surrendered without battle. They also vowed allegiance to Charles and agreed to accept baptism.

Charles was delighted with the goodwill shown by these people and ordered that the baptisms begin at once. Great wooden tubs were brought forth and filled with water. Each Saxon in turn stripped and knelt in the tub and answered certain questions of a baptismal service which had been drawn up specially for the Saxons.

"Do you foresake the devil?"

"I forsake the devil."

"And all devil worship?"

"I forsake all devil worship."

"Do you believe in God, the Father Almighty?"

"I believe in God, the Father Almighty."

"Do you believe in Christ, the Son of God?"

"I believe in Christ, the Son of God."

"Do you believe in the Holy Ghost?"

"I believe in the Holy Ghost."

No sight was more pleasing to the eyes of the "most Christian King" Charles, and no words sounded purer, but he was not able to stay to witness all the conversions because he was suddenly called away. A surprise attack had been led by the Westphalian chief Widukind at a garrison which Charles had left some twenty miles behind to protect his lines of communication and supplies.

While half of this garrison was sleeping during the heat of the day the other half had gone out foraging, and the Westphalians, like all Saxons, a very cunning people, had sent a group of their warriors to mingle with this foraging party, pretending to be part of them. This was possible because the Saxons and Franks being "first cousins" resembled each other in appearance, dress and language. Like the Franks the Saxons had blond or red hair, were clean-shaven except for a large drooping moustache and wore short tunics, woolen stockings and fur capes.

The Franks didn't noticed the strangers, and they returned to camp with the enemy in their midst. Once within the walls of the fortification, Widukind's men suddenly turned upon the Franks, slaughtering those with whom they had been foraging as well as those who were alseep. Then they swiftly disappeared.

Hearing of this disaster Charles set out in quick pursuit. He was furious at the deceit and treachery, and capturing many of the raiders, he executed them without trial.

The Westphalians now sent emissaries to Charles. They asked him to forgive them their evil ways and promised never to take up arms against him in the future. Following the example of their other Saxon brothers, they too gave

Charles hostages, swore allegiance and promised to become Christians.

Charles believed the Westphalians just as he had believed the two other Saxon tribes he had conquered. He truly believed that his barbarian neighbors now at last realized the wisdom of living in peace with the Franks and of giving up their ancient gods. He felt that their acceptance of Christianity would bind them firmly to Frankland. If the Saxons believed in the same god as the Franks, worshiped in the same manner and lived by the Ten Commandments, there would be a unity to the land.

His campaign against the Saxons had gone swiftly and well. It had lasted less than two months, and all Saxony was in submission. In a jubilant mood he wrote a letter to Hadrian telling him of his successes and of the great service he had rendered the Church. Leaving missionaries behind to attend to the mass conversions and baptisms he led his army back into Frankland.

Charles was extremely pleased with his Saxon campaign. But he was mistaken. The Saxons had deceived him with empty promises and vows. They had no idea of giving up their beloved and ancient gods. Besides, when Charles captured and executed the Westphalians who had raided his camp, their leader Widukind had escaped.

Charles hoped to spend the winter quietly with Hildegarde and his children in Frankland. Pepin the Hunchback was now a fine boy of thirteen or fourteen and Charles delighted in his company. Rothaid was beautiful and charming. Little Charles was growing out of babyhood, and Hildegarde had presented him with a second little daughter, a beautiful blond baby called Rotrud, and was expecting the birth of a fourth child. All these pleasures Charles wanted to enjoy. But his wish was not to be realized, because while he was still in Saxony he began to receive frantic messages from Pope Hadrian begging for help.

The Pope claimed that plans for a revolt in Lombardy were in the making. He warned Charles in the most urgent manner saying that Adelchis, the Lombard prince who had escaped to Constantinople after the fall of Verona, was plotting with the Dukes of Beneventum and Spoletum to recapture Lombardy. Thoroughly frightened by what he believed lay ahead, the Pope ended one of his letters with these words: "They would attack us by land and water, conquer the city of Rome and lead me into captivity. . . . Therefore I implore you by the living god and the Prince of the Apostles to hasten to our aid immediately lest we be destroyed."

The Pope's messages were frenzied and pressing, but Charles remained unmoved. He thought that Hadrian was overdramatizing the situation. In fact, he did not become alarmed until he received proof of an impending revolt from his personal representatives in Lombardy. Finally convinced that serious trouble was brewing, he acted boldly. In the dead of winter he set out for Lombardy with a small band of chosen troops, hardened fighters.

WIDUKIND THE SAXON

It was extremely dangerous for an army to cross the Alps in midwinter. The high mountain passes were blocked with snow and ice, and there was the constant danger of being buried under a crushing avalanche. But Charles was determined, and disregarding all dangers he urged his men on. He appeared fearless but was inwardly filled with apprehension, and he breathed more freely only after his men began descending the southern slopes of the Alps into the plains of Lombardy. Even then, with the snowbound and icy passes of the Alps behind them, the Franks were in grave danger, for they now found themselves confronted by a determined enemy—the people of Lombardy themselves.

While Charles and his troops had been struggling through the Alpine passes a revolt had taken place in Lombardy, and members of the old royal government had been reinstated. However, it was not the revolt which the Pope had envisioned but rather a revolt of the people. The populace had risen up against Frankish rule because of the hard conditions of life which had gripped the land since its conquest by Charles. The six months of war and the long siege of Pavia had drained the country. This, followed by a bad harvest, had resulted in a dreadful famine. Many had been reduced to dire poverty and lost their homes and farms. Whole families had been forced to give up their freedom in return for food, and fathers, mothers and children were sold into slavery in the East by unscrupulous men.

Seeing clearly why the trouble had arisen, Charles quickly

drew up a plan for rectifying his mistakes. After forcefully overthrowing the new government and reinstating pro-Frankish rulers, he began a program for relieving the appalling conditions. He traveled through Lombardy establishing contact with the distressed population and personally chose and installed capable officials to carry out measures of relief. Believing strongly that men should be free and own their own land, he ordered that those who had been forced to surrender their farms in return for food should get their lands back unless a full and proper price had been received.

During these days in Lombardy, Charles visited one city after the other. However, he carefully avoided Rome in spite of Hadrian's anxiety to see him and many urgent invitations. Charles, who was irritated by the Pope's inaccurate warnings concerning the Lombard revolt, wanted to show the Pope that he was not at his beck and call. He also feared that if he went to Rome, Hadrian might ask him to make another "Donation." Also, reports of a new revolt in Saxony had reached him; the deceitful Saxons, once he left, had not been baptized as they had promised, and they had retaken the fortress of Eresburg.

As soon as affairs in Lombardy permitted, Charles led his men back across the Alps. Taking on additional forces in Frankland, he marched straight into Saxony ready to engage in battle.

However, all opposition vanished the moment Charles

appeared on Saxon soil. The people put down their arms and said that they would willingly accept the baptism he once more insisted upon. New hostages were given and their chiefs bowed before him, once more pledging allegiance and this time vowing to forfeit their liberty and lives if they broke their word. Once more placing their hands in his they spoke those solemn words, "Great and powerful king, I shall honor and serve you faithfully for all time."

Charles was relieved that the Saxons surrendered without giving battle. But having already been deceived three times by these people, he took steps to weld them firmly to his kingdom and make certain that they would not revert again to their old pagan gods.

He divided Saxony into several districts, placing each under the rule of a churchman who was to serve not only as governor but also as a missionary, his main duty being to convert the Saxons to Christianity. The Abbot Sturm of Fulda, a monastery founded on the borders of Saxony by St. Boniface himself, was to supervise the entire program from the fortress of Eresburg.

Then to honor the Saxons and make them feel that he, Charles, King of the Franks and King of the Lombards and Patriarch of Rome, truly welcomed them as members of his realm, he ordered a royal palace and church to be built at Paderborn. That spring after they were finished he held the Field of March there, deep in the heart of Saxony, inviting all the Saxon chiefs to attend. He wanted them to share, with the other nobles and chiefs of his kingdom, in Frankish government affairs. They, too, were to have a voice.

It was a friendly and diplomatic gesture and was greatly appreciated by the Saxon chiefs. All came and bowed before Charles, once more swearing allegiance. All came and bowed except Widukind. He had escaped to Denmark and taken refuge with his brother-in-law, King of the Danes.

7

The Death of Roland

While the Field of March was in session at Paderborn during the early spring of 778, there arrived in that distant northern settlement three weary travelers. They were Mohammedans, dressed in strange Oriental clothes, and had come from far-off Spain to seek the aid of the Christian King Charles against a rival political group which had usurped power in their country.

One of these envoys was the governor of Barcelona, Al

Arabi, and he and his two companions asked Charles to send a military expedition against their enemy, the Caliph of Cordova. They said that the Mohammedan and Christian population of Spain would rise up to support him and that Berber troops from north Africa would invade southern Spain and, fighting their way north, would join with his forces. In return for his help these emissaries promised to give Charles a number of cities in northern Spain which were inhabited by Christians.

Although such an expedition would be a difficult and dangerous one, Charles was immediately attracted to the idea. He was attracted for several reasons. His grandfather, Charles the Hammer, and his father, Pepin the Short, had both fought the Mohammedans of Spain, and so it seemed fitting that he should do the same. Then too, here was a chance to save the Christians living in Spain under the rule of these infidels, these followers of Mohammed who did not believe in Christianity. Besides it would be nice to extend the borders of Frankland beyond the Pyrenees; in time one might even conquer the whole of Spain and drive the infidels out of Europe.

Legend supplies us with still one more reason why Charles wanted to go to Spain. Laying awake one night he looked up into the heavens and saw the great Milky Way overhead. He became fascinated by the idea that it seemed to rise out of his most northern province, Saxony, arch over his great realm to the south and end beyond his borders in distant Spain. He wondered if this did not have a hidden meaning.

THE DEATH OF ROLAND

Then in a vision James, the Apostle, appeared before him and revealed a deep secret. James told Charles that his body, unknown to anyone, lay buried in northern Spain. He commanded Charles to go there, conquer the land and deliver his grave from the despised infidels.

The legend goes on to say that Charles did not at first trust this dreamlike sight but that after the vision had been repeated three times he obeyed its command.

History does not record which of these reasons made Charles decide to engage in a war against the Mohammedans of Spain and which of them he used to persuade his nobles at the general assembly. It does, however, suggest that Charles realized the great difficulties of the campaign upon which he was about to engage because it is stated very clearly that he made careful plans. To avoid the torrid heat of the Spanish summer he decided to get an early start, right after Easter. He gathered together a very large army made up of troops from all parts of his vast kingdom: Lombards, Burgundians, Goths and Romans from the most southern part of Aquitaine and Franks from Neustria and Austrasia. His army even included Bavarians who were no longer under his rule but under that of his treacherous cousin, Tassilo. It is believed that they volunteered to join his expedition because of the hope of booty from rich Spain.

While waiting for his army to gather, just before Easter, Charles moved his family and court to his palace at Chasseneuil in Aquitaine not far from the city of Bordeaux. Immediately before the assembly at Paderborn, Hildegarde, who was now grown to womanhood and so beautiful that she was called Hildegarde the Fair, had given birth to her fourth child, a boy whom she and Charles named Carloman. She was now expecting a fifth child, and Charles, who loved her dearly, wanted her to be as close as possible while he was in Spain.

Charles hated being separated from his family, but when his troops finally assembled, he bid Hildegarde and his children good-by and rode forth. Seated upon a great charger he took command. With trumpets blowing, bright banners flying and a sea of lances glistening in the sun, the Frankish horde began to move toward Spain and the hope of glory.

Charles divided his army into two parts. One section he sent across the Pyrenees into eastern Spain. The other, under his personal command, marched across the Pyrenees into northwestern Spain. And from the very beginning both armies were plagued by troubles.

The population of Spain did not rise up to help Charles as the three envoys at Paderborn had promised. They fought him fiercely. Even the Christians, who had always been fairly treated by the Mohammedans, resisted his invasion; he had to storm his way into the all-Christian city of Pamplona. Neither did the Berber troops from north Africa come to his aid. And when, marching eastward to join the first half of his army, Charles arrived at the city of Saragossa on the Ebro River, he ran into insurmountable difficulties.

While Barcelona and a few other cities in northern Spain

had surrendered, Saragossa stood firm, even though it belonged to Charles' Mohammedan allies. The people of the city defied their leaders; they would have nothing to do with this Christian king from the north. They locked the gates against him, turning their walled city into an impenetrable fortress.

The capture of Saragossa was imperative to Charles' invasion of Spain, but since he had no siege machinery to attack a walled city and had food enough for only three months, he stood helpless outside its walls. In the meantime the Caliph of Cordova, his Mohammedan enemy, was gathering great forces to hurl against him.

In the face of all these difficulties there was nothing to do but retreat. Joining his two armies into one force, Charles led them back toward Aquitaine taking the same route along which he had entered Spain. And it is because of a tragic encounter which occurred during this march, on August 15, 778, that Charles' retreat from Spain has become one of the most famous retreats in all history.

The historical facts of this famous event state that as the rear guard of Charles' army was crossing the Pyrenees it was wiped out in a surprise attack by a group of local farmers and shepherds. The Gascons, as these people are known, swept down from a high mountain and, hurling themselves upon the rear guard, cut it off from the rest of the army. So sudden was the attack that the weary Franks were unable to defend themselves. All were slaughtered and the baggage train was plundered. The Gascons, who knew every rock and ravine of these rugged mountains, then disappeared leaving no trace behind. And so the Franks could not be avenged.

This is the stark account of the encounter between the Gascons and Charles' rear guard as recorded in history. But this is not the way the people of the time looked upon this tragic defeat in the rugged Pyrenees. It fired the imagination of all. It contained all the elements necessary for popular appeal: treachery, action and heroism. And at once romantic stories of the ambush began to spread through Europe, and Charles and one of his officers named Roland and Roland's friend Oliver were hailed as great heroes.

As the months passed into years these stories became more elaborate, more romantic. Minstrels took up the theme singing many versions. The bare facts were embroidered and the heroism glorified more and more through the years. And long, long after Charlemagne's death, 250 years later, these tales and ballads culminated in the greatest epic of the Middle Ages, the *Song of Roland*—a song which was sung by every minstrel and known by heart by every man, woman and child throughout the whole length and breadth of Europe, a song which served as a constant source of inspiration to the Crusaders on their way to the Holy Land.

In the *Song of Roland*, which is four thousand lines long, Roland, Governor of the Breton March or border lands between Brittany and Frankland, is presented as commander of the rear guard and as a great and noble hero and beloved nephew of King Charles. It is he who with his mighty sword, Durendal, has conquered all of Europe for Charles. He is braver than the bravest, the symbol of all knightly virtue.

The rear guard is ambushed in a narrow pass called Roncesvalles as the result of a betrayal to the enemy by a traitor called Ganelon. Roland's friend Oliver mounts a hill from which he can see the whole of Spain and a great horde of infidel Saracens.

He returns with the news that they are hopelessly outnumbered. "There are a hundred thousand of them with shields and laced helmets. . . . Roland, sound your horn; Charles will hear it and the army will return." But Roland decides to fight the enemy alone. He refuses to blow his horn to call for aid. He says, "It is better to die than to suffer the shame."

Only when twenty thousand of his men lie dead about him and he is faced with certain defeat does Roland sound his horn.

Hearing the distant call Charles starts back toward the pass at Roncesvalles.

Oliver is mortally wounded. "His heart stops beating . . . he falls full length upon the earth. . . . Roland weeps for him."

Roland returns to battle but the enemy is overwhelming, and he and all his remaining men are slaughtered. Before he dies Roland tries without success to destroy his precious sword, Durendal. He speaks to it, "It is not right that thou should fall into the hands of the heathen; you should ever be in the guardianship of Christians. May no coward ever possess you!"

Charles now arrives upon the scene. He is shaken by the ruin strewn about. The supply carts are overturned and robbed of their contents. All his men are dead, stripped of their armor and weapons. He weeps.

Coming upon Roland's body he dismounts. His grief is so great that he faints. Recovering he laments, "God lay your soul on flowers, in Paradise with all the glorious host. . . . No day shall pass henceforth that I'll not mourn. . . . Forevermore I'll reign in sorrow."

This, in brief, is the romantic version of the ambush of Charles' rear guard in the Pyrenees which has come down to us in the *Song of Roland*. But history and legend differ.

Charles returned to Aquitaine where Hildegarde awaited him with his children, including newborn twins. They were boys, and he and Hildegarde named them Lothar and Louis.

8

A Visit to Rome

Charles soon recovered from the death of his friend
Roland. However, the unsuccessful Spanish campaign and
the defeat at Roncesvalles did leave their mark upon him.
Until this campaign he had enjoyed ten years of unbroken
victories; now he had to face the fact that he was not in-
vincible and that he had lost prestige at home.

A spirit of rebellion could definitely be felt in Aquitaine.
To stem its growth Charles had to replace all local officials
with Franks whom he could fully trust.

CHARLEMAGNE

Reaching Paris he received news of further rebellion. Made bold by the fact that Charles was far off in Spain and had suffered a defeat, Widukind had returned from Denmark and stirred up his Westphalian people. They had overrun the borders of Frankland with fire and slaughter, leaving a wide path of destruction. They had burnt churches, killed priests and men, women and children, set fire to homes and destroyed crops and cattle. They had terrorized the old Abbé Sturm of Fulda and his monks, who fled into the deep woods taking with them the sacred bones of St. Boniface.

All this had been done by Widukind and his men in revenge for what Charles had done to Saxony the year before and in an attempt to throw off the heavy yoke of Christianity. The Saxons, it seemed, still loved their pagan gods.

Charles did not want to fight a winter campaign in Saxony. Besides, his men were weary of war. So in his stead he sent a small force under the command of one of his trusted nobles to subdue the Westphalians—Charles had the gift which few strong leaders have of being able and willing to delegate authority—and he disbanded the rest of the army and turned his attention to two other matters which were equally pressing.

Because so many men and horses had been taken from the farms to serve in the Spanish campaign, the harvest had been unusually small and a dreadful famine lay upon the land. Strangely enough Charles and his advisers did not understand what had caused the famine and could propose no remedy except prayer. Charles ordered that in every great church the bishop should say three masses each day: one for the king, one for the army and one for the relief of the famine.

Another problem which demanded his immediate attention was the strengthening of his rule. His kingdom was spread over such a wide area and included so many different nations with differing customs, laws and languages that he felt it would be wise to unify all these people by strengthening his central government.

He therefore spent the winter drawing up capitularies, or laws. He introduced for the first time in the Frankish realm a unified system of weights and measures. He also reformed the monetary system. Before this time there were sixty-seven localities in his kingdom that had their own mints and coinage. Each was different. Now Charles established a single system of coinage for all, a system which was later adopted in England and which survives to this day: twenty shillings to a pound of silver and twelve pennies to a shilling.

During this winter Charles also passed new laws fixing the price of grain and forbidding usury. To benefit merchants and trade he outlawed excessive highway tolls. To strengthen the Church he passed regulations forbidding the clergy and monks and nuns from marrying, entering taverns, hunting and hawking. This was necessary because in those early days it was not uncommon for priests, monks and nuns to forget their vows for a few hours or days at a time and engage in a merry hunt or frolic about at a party drinking, dancing and singing. Today men and women enter religious orders only because of deep piety, but things were different during the Middle Ages. Life was very hard, and men and women often entered religious orders seeking security. Behind monastery and nunnery walls they were safe from robbers and marauding bands and were certain of three meals a day. Parents often gave their children, especially little girls, to the Church for these reasons.

To further strengthen the Church, Charles ordered that lands which had been taken from the Church by greedy nobles should now be returned. The filing of deeds and wills was practically unknown, and so the Church had great difficulty in proving its claims to lands which had been left to it by penitents. Anyone, especially powerful nobles, could annex Church property without difficulty. And they did.

To aid the Church still more, Charles at this time also doubled the tax. He ordered that henceforth everyone should pay 20 per cent, instead of 10 per cent, of all the money he earned, of all the grain and fruits he raised and of all the increase of his flocks and herds. Everything came under this tax: honey, wax, wine, cloth, herbs, candles, everything.

It was at this period too that Charles gave more power to his *missi,* or personal representatives, who traveled through the land to see that the laws were being enforced and that justice was being done. *Missi* had existed under Pepin the Short and previous Frankish rulers, but Charles now increased their duties, their numbers and their powers.

A VISIT TO ROME

They traveled about in pairs: one a layman of high esteem and the other a bishop or abbot. They went out four times a year—in midwinter, spring, midsummer and fall—and they attended to both Church and government affairs.

The *missi* called the public together and read the king's latest decrees both in Latin and in the local dialect of the people. They investigated the conduct of churchmen and the administration of Church property and if irregularities existed they saw that they were corrected. They examined the accounts of all nobles, churches, monasteries and nunneries. They heard appeals from any, even the lowliest peasant, who felt that he had not received justice in his local courts. They checked the military supplies and the number of conscripts due the king.

The *missi* were a fine institution, and as developed by Charles they served him well. It was as though he himself were present at all times in every part of his realm.

The winter of 779–780 with its famine and revolt in Saxony was made still harder for Charles by the death of one of his little twin sons, the baby Lothar. His grief was deep and all-possessing. When spring arrived and the days grew longer and brighter with sunshine, Charles turned his thoughts toward the future. Suddenly one day he decided to go to Rome and visit the Pope.

Four years before when he was in Italy repressing the Lombard revolt he had refused to see the Pope even though Hadrian had sent him several pressing invitations; he feared that Hadrian might ask for new territory. Now Charles wanted something from Hadrian, and so with a great retinue and Hildegarde and all his children except his two eldest sons, Pepin the Hunchback and young Charles, he started forth.

Charles had two reasons for going to Rome: he was concerned about the survival of his kingdom after his death and he needed the Pope's help in settling his difficulties with his cousin Tassilo of Bavaria.

Charles' eldest son and rightful heir was Pepin the Hunchback. Charles loved this boy dearly, as did many others in the realm, for he was a forthright, intelligent and likable youth, but because of his deformity Charles felt that Pepin could never wear the crown. All kings must be strong and well-built. Only trouble could come to a land which was ruled by one who was twisted in form. There could be no doubt about it, a cripple was an evil omen; so Charles devised a plan for disinheriting Pepin and dividing his kingdom between the three sons of his beloved Hildegarde, young Charles, Carloman and Louis.

In the future there would be three kings instead of one: Carloman would be King of Italy and Louis King of Aquitaine. Young Charles would inherit all the northern part of the realm and, being the eldest of the three, would be above his brothers, holding sovereignty over their kingdoms.

Arriving in Rome Charles immediately set about putting his plan into action. To eliminate all possible future claims by Pepin the Hunchback, he asked the Pope to rechristen

Carloman and name him Pepin, the name of his revered father. He explained that it had been a mistake to name his second son Carloman after his own brother and uncle, both of whom had had such unfortunate careers.

The Pope listened to all that Charles had to say and agreed that it had been a mistake to use a name so heavily weighted with evil; names carry influences with them. He, therefore, rechristened Carloman, serving also as godfather, and thus the unfortunate Pepin, who was born with a hump on his back, was not only disinherited but robbed of his name—an insult which gnawed at his heart in the years that followed.

The first step in his plan having been accomplished, Charles now asked the Pope to crown his newly rechristened five-year-old son Pepin King of Italy, and his three-year-old son Louis, King of Aquitaine. Accordingly shortly after Easter, on April 15, 781, the two little boys were crowned and anointed by the Holy Father. Immediately following this ceremony Charles sent them with great retinues and trusted guardians to their respective kingdoms so that they might grow up among their subjects.

A description of how the baby Louis entered his kingdom has survived. In the charge of his guardian and with a whole retinue of nurses and attendants under the protection of a detachment of soldiers, he was carried in a cradle from Rome, across the Alps, to Orleans. He was then dressed in a suit of armor, fashioned for him like that of an Aquitainian noble, and placed upon a great war horse, whose reins he clutched in his tiny fists. In this manner, like a man and at the head of a retinue, did the baby king ride into his kingdom.

Hildegarde and Charles, who loved their children, were saddened at losing their two little sons. Though they planned to have the two little kings spend several months each year with them at court, they knew that their relationship would never be as close as it had been. However, the birth at this time of a little daughter named Gisla brought them some joy. Besides, Charles was soon involved in discussions with the Pope concerning his second reason for coming to Rome—Tassilo of Bavaria.

Many years before when Tassilo was fifteen he had knelt before Charles' father, Pepin the Short, and placed his hands in his and sworn to serve him and his sons Charles and Carloman as a vassal. He had sworn solemn oaths of allegiance while "touching the relics of martyrs." However, he had later broken these vows, proclaiming himself King of Bavaria, and Charles now asked the Pope to force Tassilo to live up to his pledges.

Since the breaking of such sacred oaths was a religious matter, the Pope immediately sent two envoys to Tassilo demanding that he appear in August at the national assembly of the Franks to be held at Worms. There he was to renew his vows to Charles acknowledging him as his king.

Such an order from the Pope could not be ignored, but Tassilo feared foul play and demanded that Charles guarantee his safety by giving him hostages. He was afraid that when he appeared at Worms, Charles would arrest him and force him to spend the rest of his life as a monk in some isolated monastery!

Thus far, Charles' visit to Rome had been completely successful. He had accomplished everything he had set out to do. But now the Pope, who had served Charles so well, wanted something in return, and the question of papal claims to certain lands was again revived.

Wishing to avoid any argument with the King of the Franks, Hadrian this time decided upon an ingenious plan. To prove his legal rights he showed Charles a document called the "Donation of Constantine," which it seemed had lain unnoticed for centuries under the copies of the Four Gospels on St. Peter's tomb. This document, which ran for several pages, told an interesting story. It related how Constantine, the first Christian Emperor of Rome, was afflicted with leprosy, and how after his case had been given up as hopeless, he was miraculously cured by the Bishop Sylvester of Rome.

The document continued, saying that in gratitude Constantine deeded the whole of Italy to Sylvester and to all the popes to follow him. He did even more. So that there would never be any question as to the Papacy's claims to Italy, Constantine moved the capital of his empire to the East, founding the city of Constantinople.

We do not know whether Charles believed the story or not; we know only that during the Renaissance the "Donation of Constantine" was proven to be a complete hoax. History also states that Charles remained unmoved. He had no intention of giving the Pope any of the lands that he had conquered. Neither would he recognize papal claims to the Duchies of Spoletum and Beneventum. His only concession was to offer Hadrian a small mountainous region north of Rome. Charles said that the Pope could have this area provided that he could prove beyond a question of a doubt his legal rights to it, a thing which the frustrated and fuming Pope was unable to do.

9

The Palace School

From earliest childhood Charles had displayed a passion and respect for learning. He had an extremely inquisitive mind, and wherever he went through his realm and on campaigns, he sought out scholars, musicians and artists.

He loved to converse with these men, and some of them he persuaded to join the Palace School at his court. Peter of Pisa, who taught him Latin grammar, Paul the Deacon, a poet and historian, and the learned Paulinus were three such distinguished men.

CHARLEMAGNE

The Palace School had existed at the Frankish court for many generations. Its primary purpose was to educate the sons and daughters of the Frankish kings, but the sons of nobles were also welcome. Some learned men served as teachers at the Palace School, but the learning was very limited. In fact, it was not until Charles' return from Rome in 782 that a dramatic change took place. This change can be attributed directly to the great English scholar, Alcuin, whom Charles met while he was in Italy and whom he brought home to Frankland.

Alcuin was forty-seven years old, just seven years older than Charles, and his fame for learning was well established by the time he joined the Frankish court. England was at that time the greatest seat of learning in Europe; there Latin had survived in its purest form. Alcuin, who in his own words was "always a lover of wisdom," had been educated at the Cathedral School of York by men who had sat at the feet of the Venerable Bede, the greatest scholar of his day and the author of the first history of England, a history which Alfred the Great later translated into Anglo-Saxon.

Growing to manhood Alcuin had served as the head of the Cathedral School at York, and now taking charge of the Palace School he developed it into an important factor in Frankish national life, one whose influence was to continue all through the Middle Ages. Under Alcuin at the Palace School, the fires of learning, which had been almost completely extinguished by the barbarian invasions, were fanned into flame.

THE PALACE SCHOOL

Alcuin taught in person, enlisting the aid of all the other learned men who lived at court or visited there. He sent to distant parts for books, which in those days were very rare, and to help in his work he wrote primers on writing, spelling, grammar, rhetoric and logic.

King Charles attended the school, setting an example which many of his nobles followed. This was possible because the Palace School traveled with the court from vill to vill. And while in the past only the sons and daughters of nobles had been admitted, now under Charles' order the doors were opened wide to any talented boy no matter how poor. The young men trained in this school, regardless of their background and position in life, were later used by Charles in his government and as his personal envoys.

In time another change also occurred in the Palace School. Charles and all the most learned of his court formed a sort of academy within the Palace School. Its members adopted classical names, wrote poetry and discussed literature, theology, philosophy and other subjects. Alcuin, who was first and last a theologian like all true scholars of the Middle Ages, limited his questions and answers to such learning as was encompassed by the Bible and Church writings. But Charles, while he loved nothing better than a theological debate, had a more venturesome and "modern" mind and sought the answers to such puzzles as the flight of birds and the movement of the planets.

The Palace School and the "academy" were only two of Alcuin's interests. He also served as a "Minister of Education," undertaking a national program of education. He first established schools where men could be trained as teachers. Then at the end of fifteen years when there were enough teachers, he opened free public schools throughout the realm where boys could learn the Psalms, music, chanting, arithmetic, reading and grammar. These schools were located in monasteries, and the regulations stated that "priests must receive and teach the children . . . and they are to charge no fee for their teaching and receive nothing except what the parents may offer of their own free will and love." Everyone was welcome and Charles said that his sole wish was "that all that feel the desire of learning should come freely."

However, while this rekindling of learning and the establishing of the first public school system in Europe were most remarkable for their time, very few availed themselves of the opportunity. The great masses continued in abject ignorance, unable to read or sign their names, while those who attended the schools learned little, for the quality of learning was limited.

Arithmetic and astronomy were taught primarily for ascertaining the dates of religious holidays. Classical learning was shunned and Latin was taught so that Church writings could be read and copied.

The quality of learning was indeed low. However, if the teachers and students of the realm cared for their happiness and honor they applied themselves diligently to their tasks, because King Charles, as he traveled through the land, stopped unexpectedly at even the smallest and most insignificant school to question the pupils on their studies. No one knew when the King might arrive, and woe be to those who had been idle!

At one school, finding that the sons of the nobles were not as advanced in their studies as the poorer boys, he is reported to have said, "If you think that you can trust to your birth and possessions to procure advancement, you have made a mistake. I take no account of your noble birth and your fine looks though others may admire you for them. Know this for certain, that unless you make up for your former laziness by vigorous study you will never get any favor from Charles!"

Charles, the King, was probably the most eager student in the realm. Besides being a master of Latin and understanding Greek, he studied rhetoric, logic and astronomy under Alcuin. His interest in astronomy was such that he continued its study under two Irish monks called Dungal and Clement who were attached to the school. One of his most treasured possessions was a map of the heavens made of precious metals engraved with the signs of the zodiac and the courses of the planets. He was also interested in plants and animals. And he was ever curious about distant lands and questioned all travelers and foreigners who came to his court.

He loved history and would have accounts of the past read to him while he sat at the dinner table. He was also fond of St. Augustine's books, especially *The City of God.*

He read this book, which attacks pagan thought and religion and which states that man and society can only achieve perfection through Christianity, over and over again during his lifetime.

Charles was indeed avid for knowledge. However, he was not only a student but a contributor to knowledge. He made a collection of Frankish sagas which immortalized the heroic deeds of his people. He loved music and made a collection of songs. He also began a grammar of his native Frankish tongue, the first of its kind, and gave Frankish names to the months and to the winds.

Charles' love of learning was such that he extended it beyond personal bounds. He ordered that all connected with his government study law. While he did not trust doctors, whose knowledge was confined to applying leeches, administering strange brews and recommending fasts, and preferred to administer to his own ills, he nevertheless made medicine a compulsory subject in all schools.

In an effort to make churches into cultural centers he imported builders, craftsmen and artists from Italy. In 786 he brought from Italy Roman singers whom he installed at Metz and Soissons. To these men he sent the music masters of churches throughout his land so that they might study and improve their knowledge of music. He admonished them to study diligently and to return to the pure form of the Gregorian chant, saying, "Return to the fountain of St. Gregory for you have plainly corrupted the music of the Church."

THE PALACE SCHOOL

He had Paul the Deacon compile an anthology from the works of the most honored Church Fathers to replace a volume of ill-chosen selections which had previously been used in Europe. And he addressed numerous letters to the Pope and to the many bishops and abbots of his land, stating that study and the pursuit of knowledge are essential parts of religious life and asking that they answer such questions as, "What is meant by the ritual in the baptismal service?" and, "What is the sevenfold grace of the Holy Ghost?"

No one knows what answers Charles received to these questions, but Alcuin praised his king and master for asking them, thereby "sharpening the wits of men and removing the rust of slothfulness."

The accent which Charles placed upon education had far-reaching effects, marking as it did the rebirth of general learning in Europe. However, two of its most important and specific results were the reintroduction of pure Latin into the countries north of the Alps and the creation of illuminated manuscripts.

During the first few centuries of the Christian era directly preceding the birth of Charles, Latin had fallen into a very low state; it had become corrupted by local dialects. Now under the strict surveillance of Alcuin, pure Latin was taught in the schools and reintroduced in all Church services and writings. Because Alcuin needed so many books for his schools, scriptoria were established in all monasteries. Here carefully trained monks made copies of holy writings

97

and some classical works. So that these copies would be true to the original texts no untrained person was allowed to engage in copying, as had been the case before Alcuin's arrival at court.

The copies were made on parchment and illuminated with beautifully ornamented capital letters and colored illustrations done in the most vivid colors and embellished with pure gold. The illustrations were impressive but they were surpassed by the script they used, a script which was never again equaled during the Middle Ages. It was uniform, clear and legible, and it was from this script that our modern printing and writing evolved.

Charles greatly admired this manuscript script, and there is a rather sad story connected with his attempts to master it. He knew how to write an ordinary script, but he wanted desperately to learn how to write the beautiful script which the monks had developed. He longed so to do this that Einhard tells us, "Charles used to keep tablets and blanks in bed under his pillow, that at leisure hours he might accustom his hand to form the letters. . . . However," concludes Einhard rather pathetically, "as he did not begin his efforts in due season, but late in life, they met with ill success."

10

Massacre at Verden

Late in the summer of 782 while Charles was happily occupied with Alcuin and the other scholars at his Palace
School, Widukind once more came out of hiding. Rousing
the Saxon people he again began burning churches and terrorizing the missionaries.

Charles, who did not want to be distracted from his
studies, sent an army into Saxony under the command of
three of his most trusted officers. But the Saxon revolt was
so widespread and intense that this force proved insufficient,

99

and he soon had to send reinforcements under the command of Theoderic, a close relative.

The two Frankish armies joined on the banks of the Weser in the heart of Saxony and marched forward together to engage the Saxons, who had withdrawn to a fortified position on the slopes of a mountain called Suntal. However, jealousy on the part of the three original Frankish commanders against Theoderic destroyed all hope of victory.

In the battle that followed, the Franks were overwhelmed and cut down. Only a few escaped.

When the news of the terrible defeat reached Charles he was gripped with rage, not only against his selfish and jealous commanders, but also against Widukind and the "obstinate," "deceitful" Saxons who had repeatedly broken their solemn oaths to him over the past ten years. Determined to put an end to Saxon resistance once and for all, he marched north at the head of a large army. As usual, the news of his coming had traveled before him, and when Charles reached the Weser no trace could be found of Widukind and the fighting men who had made up his strong forces. All had vanished.

The Saxons had disappeared in this manner before and Charles had always been tolerant, but this time his patience was at an end. He was determined to capture the leaders, so he issued an order for all Saxon nobles to come to him at Verden, a settlement on the Weser not far from present-day Bremen. When they had gathered he demanded that they surrender the leaders to him.

They all blamed Widukind. They said that they had not supported Widukind in any way. In fact, they said that they were solidly against Widukind because they felt his cause was hopeless and because he had broken a most ancient Saxon custom and led the people into war without first getting permission to do so at the national assembly of Saxon chiefs held each year to decide such questions.

What they said was true, but Charles, who was still in a state of fury, would not believe that they were all innocent and that there was only one leader. He insisted that others be produced, and was so vehement in his demand that the Saxon chiefs began to fear for their heads. In a state of panic they denounced each other and many of the common people.

All who were denounced were seized and brought to Verden. And in a single day 4500 men were massacred in cold blood.

Having gained his revenge Charles now returned to Frankland to be with Hildegarde, who was expecting her ninth child. But Charles who had brought sorrow to so many homes in Saxony was now himself to know its full meaning.

On April 30, 783, Hildegarde died in childbirth. The infant girl, who was named after her, survived only a few weeks. Then three months later Charles also lost his devoted mother, Queen Bertrada.

Queen Bertrada was buried beside her husband, Pepin the Short, in a great ceremony at the Abbey of St. Denis, but

Hildegarde, the "mother of kings," was buried at the Church of St. Arnulf's at Metz not far from the royal palace at Thionville on the Moselle River. Paul the Deacon wrote her epitaph praising her beauty and accomplishments and ending with the words: "Here lies the most virtuous queen Hildegarde, wife of Charles the most powerful king."

Everyone had loved Hildegarde, and she was deeply mourned. In her honor Charles deeded a great estate to St. Arnulf's. He did this warning the abbot and his successors, on the pain of punishment from God, never until the end of time to use the profits from this estate for any purpose other than for masses and prayers for the repose of Hildegarde's soul and for candles for the sepulcher of this his "most beloved wife."

Charles was crushed by the death of Hildegarde. They had been married for thirteen years and she had borne him four sons and five daughters, and he had loved her dearly. But immediately after her funeral he was forced to repress his grief and lead his army back into Saxony because the brutal butchery at Verden had brought about still one more Saxon revolt.

Verden had so shocked the Saxons that now the whole country was united against Charles. Widukind was the leader, and this time a single campaign would not bring Charles his victory. The Saxons were to fight him in a hard and bitter war which was to last for three long years—a war during which young Charles, who was now thirteen, was for the first time given the command of troops.

MASSACRE AT VERDEN

Frankish annals claim that during this three-year war, Charles won one victory after another; however, historical records indicate that this was not the case and that every inch of ground was fiercely contested. There were several bloody battles during the first year, one of which was fought with such "fierce wrath" that its site was known for generations after as the "Hill of Slaughter." During the second year the situation was so serious that Charles could not go home for Christmas, and Fastrada, the daughter of an Austrasian count whom he had recently married because a king must have a queen, together with all his children and members of his court, were forced to travel the icy roads into the wilderness of Saxony to be with him for the Holy Days.

It was, indeed, not until the third year that, as Frankish annals state, "no man could stop him and he went where he would through Saxony." However, Widukind had not yet been captured, and Charles dared not relax. Widukind had escaped across the Elbe into the lands of wild north Saxon tribes where he had many devoted followers. If these tribes decided to fight, the war could continue for still another year. Charles knew this and so did Widukind. But both of them also knew something else.

The Saxons, upon whose soil the war was being waged, had suffered the most, of course. Their villages and farms had been burned. Their cattle and fields destroyed. But the Franks had also suffered. The war had drained manpower from the whole realm. Food and other supplies were short. On both sides the people were grumbling, and Charles and

Widukind each realized that some sort of peace must be arranged.

Charles, who held the superior position, was the first to act. He sent some Saxons, whom he had captured in battle, as emissaries to Widukind. And Widukind, confronted by the hopelessness of the whole situation, consented to deal with him. Demanding hostages as a guarantee of his safety, Widukind agreed to go into Frankland to see Charles.

The hostages were given, and shortly thereafter Widukind appeared at Charles' court at Attigni, where he promised not only to give up his fight but also to accept baptism.

The overjoyed Charles stood beside Widukind when he received baptism, hearing him pronounce the words, "I forsake the devil and all devil worship. . . . I believe in God, the Almighty Father. . . . I believe in Christ, the Son of God. . . . I believe in the Holy Ghost."

Charles now showered Widukind with gifts and allowed him to return to Saxony, where it is recorded he lived till the end of his life, many many years later. He was true to his word and never again roused his people to revolt against the Franks.

Charles' conferences with Widukind had been conducted in a civilized and generous spirit, but now that Saxony was his, Charles allowed his anger against the Saxons to once more dictate his actions. Against the counsel of Alcuin and all his other government advisers and under the influence, some believe, of Fastrada, who was an extremely cruel woman, he issued a very severe "Capitulary on Saxony."

MASSACRE AT VERDEN

The Saxons were not to live under their old laws and ancient customs as did the other peoples in Charles' realm such as the Lombards, Burgundians and Aquitainians. The Saxons were, henceforth, to live under special laws, and they were to accept Christianity or suffer death; they must renounce their ancient gods, and every man, woman and child must be baptized. The Church was to conduct the courts of justice and hold the power of life and death over the people.

So severe were Charles' laws for Saxony that there were at least fifteen crimes punishable by death. Most of these crimes were offenses against the Church. Even eating meat during Lent was considered a capital crime. The people were also forced to pay a tithe to the Church.

Charles' Capitulary on Saxony was so cruel that it verged on being inhuman. In it he displayed a brutality which was not characteristic of him and certainly not to be commended. Yet many historians believe that he also displayed genius in first placing this heavy yoke upon the Saxons and then giving the Church the sole right to remove it. Since churchmen were the only ones who could forgive the people their crimes and save them from death, it followed that the survival of the people lay in supporting the Church in every way and living on the friendliest terms with all churchmen.

11

Bavaria

During the three years that Charles was engaged in the Saxon war he received a continuous flow of troublesome messages from Pope Hadrian. These letters dwelt with boring repetition on only one subject: the Pope claimed that the Duke of Beneventum, Tassilo of Bavaria and the Empress Irene in Constantinople were planning to join forces to crush Charles' growing power in Europe.

Charles was not alarmed by the Pope's warnings because

he felt that Hadrian was probably as inaccurate and exaggerated in his fears as he had been concerning the Lombard revolt. He suspected that what Hadrian really wanted was to get him to come to Rome so that he could make some new territorial demands upon him. Still, certain facts could not be denied.

Firstly, while Charles was engaged in Saxony, Tassilo had again broken his sacred vows of allegiance by building up a strong armed force and plotting with the Avars, a barbaric Mongolian tribe on his eastern borders, to join him against Charles in the event of war. Secondly, Irene, who had recently poisoned her husband, the Emperor, and was acting as regent for her ten-year-old son Constantine, was a very evil person capable of joining any plot. Besides, Adelchis, the Lombard prince who had escaped from Verona many years before, was living at her court and trying to foment trouble. Thirdly, Tassilo's wife and the wife of the Duke of Beneventum, who were daughters of the deposed King of Lombardy and sisters of Adelchis and of Charles' castoff queen Desiderata, were eager for revenge against him.

Yes, the Pope might be inaccurate and exaggerating, still. . . . Carefully weighing the inherent dangers of these three sources of future trouble, Charles decided to act. He could do nothing against Irene in far-off Constantinople. Neither could he declare war on Tassilo, because the three years of Saxon war had drained his realm very low. His people would not tolerate another full-scale war so soon;

there was ugly grumbling among his nobles. And so he settled upon a scheme by which he hoped to eliminate two of his enemies at one blow and strike fear into the hearts of any others who might be plotting against him. He decided to strike against the Duke of Beneventum, who was weak and could, therefore, be easily overcome. While in Italy he would visit the Pope and gain his help in eliminating his disloyal cousin Tassilo and in bringing Bavaria directly under his rule.

Having thus made up his mind, Charles started out at once for Italy with a small military force. It was midwinter and the snows were deep, but he crossed the dangerous Alps without difficulty.

He spent Christmas in Florence, then went on to Rome where he was received by the Pope with a great display of ceremony and friendship. Hadrian had heard that Charles had come to Italy to invade the Duchy of Beneventum, and his hopes were high. Perhaps now he might gain some of those lands and cities the Papacy coveted so keenly.

Hadrian's dreams were taking on the glow of reality, but they were quickly shattered. The Duke of Beneventum, learning of Charles' arrival in Rome, was seized with fear and immediately sent his eldest son, Romuald, to beg Charles not to invade his duchy and to assure him of his loyalty. As proof of his sincerity he had instructed Romuald to offer himself to Charles as a hostage and to say that he would raze the walls of all the fortified places in Beneventum and that he and all the other men in his land would cut off their long flowing beards!

The Frankish nobles who were with Charles and his armed force, inspired by thoughts of rich booty, were eager for war. The Pope, who had his own dreams of gain, was also eager. But Charles decided otherwise. He liked the young Romuald, who was a cultured and intelligent youth, so much that he forgave his father, the Duke, for his part in the alleged plot against him and accepted the Duke's terms—beards and all.

He asked for only two further concessions—that the Duke of Beneventum and all his people swear a personal vow of allegiance to him and pay an annual tribute. Then unable to bear the thought of how he, himself, would feel if he had to give as hostage such a son as Romuald, he sent the young man back to his father, asking for a younger son as a substitute hostage.

The Pope was furious at Charles for having treated the Duke of Beneventum so kindly. How could he do this, the Pope argued, when everyone knew he was one of those lawless Lombards who was holding territory which rightfully belonged to the Papacy. To appease His Holiness, Charles gave the Pope another "Donation," Capua and several other cities. But as before, this "Donation" also depended upon the Pope's being able to prove that he had a previous valid claim!

Under the circumstances Charles' gift to the Pope was

hardly a gift at all. But that did not deter Charles from asking Hadrian for something in return. He asked that the Pope at once condemn Tassilo and hurl upon him all the churchly punishments within his power.

"The whole earth," it was recorded at the time, "rang with the news of Tassilo's treachery." In an effort to defend himself, Tassilo sent two envoys to Rome to plead his cause with Hadrian.

Tassilo was a good Christian and well liked by the Pope. He had sent missionaries into the land of his neighbors, the Avars, to bring the word of God to those barbaric Mongolian people, and he had always been very generous with gifts to the Church. And so the Pope weighed the charges against him carefully.

He held many meetings with Charles and Tassilo's two representatives. He was anxious that there should be no miscarriage of justice. However, when Tassilo's envoys were unable to explain their lord's behavior, Hadrian finally gave in to Charles' demands. He found Tassilo guilty of having again broken his sacred vow of allegiance, and he ordered him to submit at once to his lord Charles, King of the Franks and of the Lombards. Should Tassilo fail to do so, he and all his Bavarian subjects were to suffer the curse of excommunication and eternal damnation.

Well satisfied with the result of this, his third visit to Rome, Charles set out for Worms in the heart of Frankland, where Fastrada and his children awaited him. Immediately upon his arrival he summoned his nobles to a general assembly to be held in that city in the fall.

Tassilo was summoned along with the rest. As one of Charles' vassals it was his duty to attend, but when everyone was assembled it was noted that he was missing.

In an impassioned speech Charles asked the assembly to declare war, but his nobles hesitated. They wanted to give Tassilo one more chance. However, when news reached Worms that Tassilo was at that very moment massing troops, they gave Charles their consent. Such contempt could not go unpunished.

Charles lost no time. He organized an army and marched toward Bavaria. However, the war never took place, because while Tassilo was indifferent to the Pope's curse, his subjects were not. The Bavarian people were panic-stricken at the thought of eternal damnation. His troops refused to march. And Tassilo was forced to submit.

There at the border of his country he appeared before Charles. Kneeling he kissed the King's knee and, placing his hands in Charles', swore undying allegiance for the third time. He humbled himself still further—he surrendered his duchy by handing Charles his staff of authority. This was a wooden scepter carved with the head of a man, the ancient Frankish symbol of possession.

Charles was satisfied. In a gesture of generosity and before all the Bavarian nobles who were with Tassilo, he restored the duchy to Tassilo by returning the staff. Then to show that all was forgiven, he gave Tassilo many gifts, including a suit of armor, a horse with a blanket of gold cloth and a large estate on the Bavarian border.

As a guarantee of his good faith Tassilo gave Charles a number of hostages, including one of his sons. But Tassilo had evil in his heart. As soon as he was safely home he began to plot a rebellion. He expelled all the representatives of King Charles who were in Bavaria and appealed to the Avars for help. This last act was a fatal mistake, for his nobles, rather than allow the pagan Avars into their land, denounced him to King Charles.

Charles' anger had now reached the point of rage, but he controlled himself and kept the information secret. However, when Tassilo appeared at the Field of March the following year he was immediately arrested. A detachment of Frankish soldiers was already on its way to Bavaria to seize his wife and their children.

In the trial that followed, Tassilo was accused of treason by one Bavarian noble after another. He made no attempt to defend himself, admitting everything and asking only for mercy. The verdict was death.

However, Charles once more displayed his leniency toward his treacherous cousin. He commuted the sentence, ordering instead that Tassilo and his entire family take religious vows. Tassilo and his two sons had their heads shaved. Liutperga and his daughters took the veil. All were condemned for life to monastery and nunnery.

With the annexation of Bavaria to the Frankish realm all

the Germanic people of Europe were now under one rule. With the annexation of Bavaria the German nation was born. A milestone of history had been reached.

However, the acquisition of Bavaria had still another important aspect; with the conquest of this land Charles became master of all civilized Europe with the exception of the British Isles, Spain and the extreme southern part of Italy. The Mediterranean, which had once been a Roman sea, was now flanked by three great powers: Charles' Frankish kingdom in the north, the Byzantine Empire in the east and the Arab Empire in the south.

12

The Avars

Having at last realized his wish to bring Bavaria under his direct rule, Charles longed to return to the peace and the pleasures of his court. He was now forty-six years old and was beginning to tire of war. He wanted to spend his days with his wife and children and with Alcuin and the other scholars at the Palace School. Besides, young Charles, Louis, King of Aquitaine and Pepin, King of Italy, were in need of training in diplomacy and other kingly tasks. Louis, who spent so much time in rich, luxury-loving Aquitaine, was in special need of guidance; he was entirely too meek and easily influenced.

Charles also wanted to devote himself to a new interest. Ever since his first visit to Rome, thirteen years before, he had dreamed of someday building a new Rome in the heart of Frankland, just as the Emperor Constantine had built a new capital for himself in the East. This new Rome would serve as the capital of his realm and as his permanent residence. There would be a great marble palace and a magnificent chapel, and all would be in a splendor befitting a great king.

Charles had chosen the site. He would build his capital on ground now occupied by a small royal vill at Aachen in beautiful rolling country between the Meuse and the Rhine River. He loved this spot because it was true Frankish country and the home of his ancestors. Besides, it was well located. It was midway between the cities of Cologne and Liege and only some sixty miles from where he was constructing a great bridge of wood on stone piers across the Rhine, to give him and his armies easy access to the north.

Once he decided upon the location for his new Rome, he pushed ahead with his plans with his usual energy. Einhard, who had been brought up with his children, attended the Palace School and become a member of the "academy," was Charles' architect and had already drawn up plans. Materials had been collected, and the Pope promised to send marble from Rome. Since the people of Europe were very crude builders, Charles had gathered skilled workmen from Italy and Constantinople, and they were already at work.

Aachen was the dream of his heart, and it was this project to which Charles now wanted to devote most of his time. But there was a pressing problem which prevented him from having his wish; Charles felt that his realm was not safe as long as the wild pagan Avars, who had been in league with Tassilo, remained unchallenged on his far eastern border.

He decided that the Avars must be conquered and subjugated, so he immediately began making plans for war. Recalling his many troublesome campaigns in Saxony, he decided that this time he would strike with such force that the matter would be decisively settled once and for all. He therefore asked the general assembly to give him a force as large as that which he had taken to Spain and made up of troops from all parts of his realm.

The Avars were a strange fierce people who had come out of Central Asia toward the end of the sixth century. They were big men, Mongols, with yellow skin, high cheekbones, slanting eyes and broad noses. And they wore their hair in long pigtails.

The arrival of the Avars on the eastern border of Europe struck terror into the weakened Roman Empire. When they threatened to attack Constantinople, the Emperor Justinian immediately offered to pay them a high yearly tribute which, with some variations, was still being paid some 250 years later by the Empress Irene. Besides spices, silks and jewels it often included as much as 100,000 gold coins.

The Avars were originally a nomad people, but reaching the fertile valley of the Danube they gave up their wandering life. Settling down in those lands which we know today as Hungary and Yugoslavia they devoted themselves to farming, to raiding the territory of their neighbors to the west and to threatening Constantinople in order to keep the tribute flowing.

The several tribes which made up the Avars lived in settlements which were protected by great circular earth embankments or rings. The chief of the Avars, or *Khakan,* lived in the largest ring of all. It was made up of nine concentric rings of embankments and covered an immense area. The rings were widely spaced, some as much as twenty miles apart, and whole villages and farms existed between them. To go from one ring to another, one went through narrow passages which could be easily barricaded. In the very center of this great circular maze was the Khakan's palace and the immense treasure which the Avars had collected from Constantinople during the past two-and-a-half centuries.

Early in the year 791, Charles sent an ultimatum to the Khakan of the Avars demanding that he stop molesting Christians and that he end all raids on the eastern borders of the Frankish realm. As Charles expected, this demand was ignored, so he gave orders for his forces to advance. He had three separate armies: one would attack from Lombardy, one from the west and one from the north.

CHARLEMAGNE

The Avars were excellent horsemen and bowmen and in spite of their primitive method of warfare proved a very difficult enemy. However, the first attack against them, which came from Lombard troops under the command of Charles' fourteen-year-old son Pepin, was a complete success.

In a rare document, the only intimate letter written by Charles that has survived, he proudly describes this encounter to his queen, Fastrada. He writes:

> A messenger from our beloved son, Pepin, reports that . . . Almighty God, in His mercy gave the victory to him and his Lombard troops and that they killed many Avars; never before, even in long battles, have so many of the enemy fallen. Our men stormed their camp, which was protected by a wall, and stayed there all night and the next day. . . . They then left weighed down with spoils. . . . They took 150 Avar prisoners.

Charles now advanced and, joining with Bavarian troops which came down from the north, entered Avar territory. Seeing his overwhelming force the Avars abandoned their first line of defense in what is today known as the Vienna Woods. Many in their confusion surrendered. Many more were slain.

However, this first success was not to be repeated so easily by Charles. In the weeks that followed the Avars put up very stiff resistance. There were many bloody en-

118

counters, and while Charles conquered half their land before the arrival of winter, the Avars were by no means defeated. It would take seven years to do that.

With the arrival of winter Charles left his troops under the command of trusted officers and went to his palace at Regensburg in Bavaria not far from the theater of war. There Fastrada and his children, including Louis of Aquitaine, awaited him. While Pepin had distinguished himself in the Avar war, Louis, who was soft and had the "soul of a monk," had proven a great disappointment. During the encounter in the Vienna Woods he had shown himself unfit for battle, and Charles had been forced to send him home.

In the spring Charles planned to rejoin his army, but a number of problems prevented him from doing so. In fact, he never again personally commanded troops in the Avar war. He did, however, follow its progress with intense interest, and he ordered a bridge of boats to be built across the Danube so that his troops and supplies would have easy passage.

There were several problems which prevented Charles from returning to the Avar war, but the two which worried him most concerned the Church. There was unrest in Saxony and an outbreak of heresy in Spain and Aquitaine. In spite of his treatment of the Pope, Charles was a very pious man who considered himself as defender of the Church and felt that it was his duty to devote all his energies to these matters. Besides he knew that the Church served as a unifying force in his vast realm; the many different peoples he ruled were bound together by their common belief in Christ. They shared one God, and all worshiped in one manner. He had no intention of permitting the Saxons to return to their old gods or of letting an heretical doctrine destroy this unity and thus weaken his rule.

At the end of the Saxon war Charles had been warned by Alcuin and his other advisers not to impose such strict laws upon the Saxons. Alcuin had said that "newly converted people must be treated like children," with gentleness, otherwise they would revert to their old beliefs. He had also cautioned Charles against forced baptism, saying, "What is the use of baptism without faith? A man can be forced to baptism but not to believe." He and other advisers had warned Charles particularly against making these people, impoverished by a long war, pay a tithe to a Church for which they held no love. Charles had not heeded their words, and now the helpless people of Saxony were resisting Christianity and chafing under the oppression of his heavy hand.

Alcuin again advised Charles to lighten the burden of this conquered people, but Charles refused to do so. In fact he now added to their misery by personally leading troops into Saxony to discipline the restless Saxons and force them to abide by his unjust laws. To make them realize that he was master he resorted to a very cruel measure. He deported hundreds of men, women and children to distant parts of his realm.

His treatment of the Saxons was pitiless, but one thing of

great interest happened at this time. He conceived a plan for forming a water route linking the North Sea with the Danube. After consulting with men who were said to know about such things, he decided to dig a canal linking a tributary of the Danube to a tributary of the Main, which flows into the Rhine, which in turn flows into the North Sea. Such a canal would facilitate his moving troops and matériel between his two theaters of war—the land of the Avars and Saxony—and when the wars were over would be very advantageous for trade.

Work was begun at once. Charles and his entire court, which had moved up for the occasion, watched as thousands of men with picks and spades dug a great ditch almost a mile long and more than 250 feet wide and carted the soil and rocks away in baskets and ox-drawn wagons.

But the rains came, unusually heavy rains, and the whole project turned into a sea of mud. It had to be abandoned. However, a scar on the earth can still be seen there today, and a little village called Graben, or "ditch," stands close by reminding the visitor of a time long ago and of a man's dream.

Having attended to the Saxon problem, Charles now turned his attention to heresy in Spain and Aquitaine. It had started when Bishop Elipand of Toledo, an old man of almost eighty, came to the conclusion after years of studying the Gospels that Christ was not the natural Son of God but a mortal and therefore the adopted Son of God. He explained his theory to a friend, Bishop Felix of Urgel, who was immediately won over and began to give the idea circulation even though it was in direct contradiction to Church doctrine and therefore heretical. It not only denied the Virgin birth but came close to denying the divinity of Christ.

The Adoptionist Heresy, as it came to be known, spread with amazing rapidity in Spain and crossed the border into Aquitaine. Bishops, priests and monks as well as the people made it their own. Thousands upon thousands accepted it as truth. The Pope condemned the doctrine, calling it blasphemous and serpent's venom, but still it continued to spread.

It was at this critical moment that Charles, realizing that words of condemnation would not stem the growth of this heresy, decided to act. The town of Urgel was in his Spanish March, and so he was free to demand that Bishop Felix appear before a court of bishops at his palace at Regensburg and present his case.

The verdict was, of course, against Felix. His heresy was condemned and books written by him and the old Bishop Elipand were ordered burned.

Felix bowed to his fate and promised to go back to his diocese and amend the evil which he had caused. However, Charles did not trust him and sent him instead to Rome under guard so that the Pope might deal with him. There the penitent Felix wrote a paper against his theory of adoptionism. In the presence of the Pope he placed it upon the sacred tomb of St. Peter. Then swearing that he would evermore believe that Christ was the real Son of God and not the adopted Son of God, he was allowed to return to Urgel.

The vows which Felix made to Charles and the Pope appeared to be sincere, but as soon as he was back in Urgel he stubbornly reverted to his heresy, preaching it with more fervor than ever. Charles was enraged. He decided to try Felix once more at a great Church council in Frankfurt. It would counteract the Council of Nicaea which the Empress Irene had recently held and at which image worship had been pronounced as an acceptable practice for the entire Christian Church.

Charles disapproved of image worship. The early churches of his realm had been unadorned except for crosses, and he deplored the increasing practices of decorating church walls with holy pictures and of placing statues of Christ, the Virgin and the saints in churches and at roadsides where people could stop and pray. He felt that the people were thus being encouraged to revert to the pagan practice of idol worship. Besides he wanted Irene to know that he, Charles, King of the Franks and Lombards and Patriarch of Rome, was master of the Church in Rome and everywhere else in Europe and that he would tolerate no interference from Constantinople.

And so on June 1, 794, he convened the Council of Frankfurt. Frankfurt was at that time nothing more than a tiny wilderness settlement, yet the gathering which took place there was colorful and dramatic. The great hall built of dark

123

rough-hewn logs glowed with the light of candles and torches. It was brightened by the brilliant reds, purples, gold and dazzling whites of the robes of the many archbishops and bishops, who had come together with priests, deacons and other more lowly churchmen. There were even two personal representatives of the Pope in their most resplendent gowns.

Charles, the self-appointed defender and head of the Church, presided over the council. He opened the proceedings by directly attacking image worship. He spoke with passion and conviction and, being a most powerful speaker, immediately won many to his side. Then presenting the council with several volumes which he had written on the subject and which are known to us as the *Caroline Books*, he rested his case.

Charles liked nothing better than a theological debate. For years past, he had engaged in such debates with all the most learned churchmen of his realm, including the Pope. His attack on image worship as presented in the *Caroline Books* quickly convinced all who were gathered at Frankfurt, even those who had previously sided with Irene, and image worship was condemned.

Satisfied that he had won his battle against Irene, Charles now returned to the problem of the Adoptionist Heresy. The Bishop Felix was brought forward and questioned. After careful consideration of all aspects of his case, and in accordance with Charles' wishes, he was unanimously condemned and warned that "if he persisted in his error" he would be excommunicated and suffer eternal damnation.

But even these dire threats did not stop the stubborn Felix from preaching what he firmly believed. A few years later Charles was forced to hold still another trial and force him to recant once more. This time, however, Charles did not allow Felix to return to Urgel. He sent him to Lyons, ordering the bishop of that diocese to keep him there for the rest of his life and to see that he did not revert to his evil ways.

In order to wipe out the effects of Felix's heresy Charles sent a delegation of churchmen into Aquitaine and the Spanish March to call back to the true faith all those who had faltered. It was a gigantic task but their efforts were successful. Since Bishop Elipand was now much too old to carry on the fight alone, the Adoptionist Heresy also disappeared in Spain.

Charles had saved the unity of the Church in Europe.

The war against the Avars continued while Charles was engaged with these troublesome Church matters, and in the fourth year the Frankish forces under the command of Eric, Duke of Friuli, won a great victory. The Avars, weary of such a long struggle, began to fight among themselves; one rebellious faction murdered the Khakan. Taking advantage of the unrest Eric was able to penetrate the great ring, reaching its very core where the treasure was hidden.

It took fifteen wagons, each drawn by four oxen, to bring the Avars' treasure into Frankland; and when Eric arrived at Aachen where Charles and his court were now established in the magnificent new palace, the excitement was over-whelming. No one had ever seen so much gold, so many silk robes and hangings, so many dazzling jewels, silver and gold cups and bowls, magnificent glass vases and goblets, swords with hilts of precious metals, richly ornamented bridles, saddles and stirrups.

Charles was a generous person and distributed this booty in a most extravagant manner. He scattered the gold coins over his realm, rewarding everyone who had ever served him—nobles and soldiers, the servants on his many estates, bishops, abbots and priests—all received a share. An appropriately large portion was sent to Hadrian in Rome, and even King Offa of England received a gift.

Einhard was present when the treasure of the Avars arrived at Aachen. He tells us, "No war in which the Franks have ever engaged within the memory of man brought them such riches and such booty." He was not exaggerating, because the distribution by Charles of so much gold through his realm caused an inflation. The price of grain and other foods and commodities rose so rapidly that the economy was upset.

With Eric's penetration of the great ring, Avar resistance began to crumble. Young Pepin and his Lombard troops were able to make great advances, and before long he too was able to break into the ring, where he found still more of the treasure which the Avars had accumulated over 250 years.

Pepin leveled the Khakan's palace and laid waste all the

farms and fortifications within the great ring. Then he proudly led a train of treasure-laden wagons to his father in Aachen. Once more Charles generously shared his good fortune and unintentionally aggravated the inflation that already gripped the realm.

However, it seems the people were willing to overlook whatever discomfort this inflation caused them, for it was at this time that Charles first began to be called "the Great." They began to speak of him as Carolus Magnus, Charle–Magne, Charlemagne. No other ruler, before or since, has been called "the Great" during his lifetime.

With the destruction of the Khakan's ring the Avar war came to a close. The fighting had been so fierce and the devastation so widespread during the seven years of conflict that only a scattered few Avars survived. They moved out of their territory and were absorbed by the people of the lands into which they went before Charles could put into effect a plan he had for converting them all to Christianity. They disappeared so completely that they became one of the lost peoples of history and a proverb arose which is still commonly used by Slavic people today, "To disappear like the Avars."

13

Pepín the Hunchback

During the years between the end of the Saxon war and the arrival in Aachen of the Avar treasure, during the years when Charles was disciplining the restless Saxons and fighting the Adoptionist Heresy, the entire length and breadth of his great kingdom was troubled by unrest and discontent. And a plot developed against the life of Charles, the once much loved King of the Franks.

The three-year war in Saxony had reduced the economy

to a dangerous level. His was a purely agricultural society, and so many men and horses had been drafted that the harvests were small and the land threatened by a hidden enemy—hunger. Charles and his advisers had no knowledge of economics. They were ignorant of the simplest rules of supply and demand, and so without waiting for the realm to recover from the strain of the Saxon war, Charles declared war upon the Avars.

For this war he amassed the largest army he had had since the days of his disastrous Spanish campaign. He drafted great numbers of men and horses from every part of his realm. The countryside was depleted of laborers. And when at the end of the first year a plague struck the horses, killing thousands upon thousands, the economic balance was completely upset and the inevitable occurred. Just as in the year following the Spanish campaign a dreadful famine gripped every part of the land. The people in the warm climates of Lombardy and Aquitaine, where food was normally plentiful, suffered as much as those in the north. Many freemen in desperation became serfs, giving up their farms and freedom in exchange for food. Noble and peasant alike tasted the empty bitterness of hunger. And since hunger always breeds discontent, discontent was voiced openly everywhere. Hostility and treason were in the air.

The nobles, who were directly responsible for supplying contingents for the army, felt the weight of the economic imbalance more than any other class. But when they complained that they could not spare any more men from their districts, Charles would not listen. In fact, he behaved in a most unreasonable manner. He demanded that they fill their quotas anyway, and to hold them strictly to account he increased the visits of his missi. Any noble or freeman who tried to evade his duty, regardless of the reason, had to pay a heavy fine.

The nobles were angry and puzzled by Charles' severity; always in the past he had been reasonable and just with them, and they suspected that the hardhearted Queen Fastrada was behind it. Regardless of what caused the change in him, they decided they had to do something to free themselves from such tyranny.

The conspiracy against Charles was organized by a few nobles, and it centered in his court. Their plan was to kill Charles and his three heirs and place Pepin the Hunchback upon the throne. They felt that this prince, once he was king, could easily be managed.

In Pepin the Hunchback the conspirators found a willing tool, because although this eldest son of Charles had always lived in the palace and been loved by his father, he harbored deep resentments. He had been brought up by three step-mothers; and unhappy about his deformity, humiliated because his mother had been divorced, angered because he had been barred from his rightful inheritance, embittered by the fact that his name had been given to a younger brother, he was easily persuaded to join the plot. One night he secretly left the palace and met with the conspirators in a nearby church.

PEPIN THE HUNCHBACK

A Lombard monk called Fardulf, who was a poet and had therefore become a friend of the King's, who encouraged all arts and learning, happened to be in the church at the time. Seeing a group of high nobles and the hunchback prince entering so late at night, Fardulf wondered at the reason. Hiding behind the altar, he overheard everything that was said.

Crouching in his hiding place, Fardulf did not stir. As long as he stayed perfectly still he felt that he would be safe. But he was wrong. The conspirators, now that all had been discussed, suddenly became fearful that someone might have overheard them, and rushing about the church in a frantic search, they discovered Fardulf and dragged him from his hiding place.

The terrified monk expected to be killed on the spot, but his life was spared. The conspirators thought that because he was a Lombard, one of a conquered people, he too bore Charles a grievance. So they simply asked him to swear that he would not disclose their plot.

White with fear Fardulf swore by all that was holy to protect their secret. But as soon as the conspirators left the church he ran to the palace and, in spite of the lateness of the hour, demanded to see the King.

In the bedchamber he fell to his knees and told Charles all that had happened. Within a few hours Pepin the Hunchback and the other conspirators were under arrest.

In the trial that followed, all, including Pepin the Hunchback, were condemned to death. However, Charles, who loved all his children, including his deformed son Pepin, could not bear to lose him in spite of what had happened. So he commuted his sentence.

Pepin's head was shaved and he was sent off to the monastery of Prum not far from Aachen. There in prayer and meditation Pepin the Hunchback spent the rest of his life.

Immediately after the trial the conspirators met their deaths. Some were hanged, others beheaded, but Charles was not satisfied. He had been badly shaken, and he ordered an investigation to be conducted throughout his realm in order to discover if any others were plotting against him.

When the investigation was over and he felt reassured, he held a royal assembly where he rewarded all those who were loyal to him. He gave them gold and other valuable presents. Fardulf, the monk, received the finest present of all. Charles made him Abbot of St. Denis, that great and wealthy monastery outside Paris, where his grandfather, Charles the Hammer, and his father and mother, Pepin the Short and Bertrada, lay buried.

Fardulf was so grateful that he built a royal guesthouse at St. Denis so that King Charles and his court could come and stay whenever he chose.

14

The Royal Palace at Aachen

While Charles was beset by the troubles of the Adoptionist Heresy and the plot against his life, and just before the Avar war drew to a close, Queen Fastrada, who had always been sickly and ailing, suddenly died. She had not been liked at court because she was a cruel woman and had a bad influence on Charles. During the years of their marriage he deviated from his usual kindness and tolerance, displaying a harsh and cruel nature. Immediately after her death, it has been noted by some who knew him, he returned to his natural gentleness.

It can be assumed that Charles was not happy with Fastrada for there is no record that he grieved very deeply at her death. In fact, he married for a fifth time shortly after her death. This time he married a beautiful young girl called Liutgard, who was loved by everyone because she was not only beautiful and charming but also kind and gentle, "doing good to all and working harm to none."

Liutgard made a perfect companion for Charles. Although she was very young and he was now fifty-two, with a flowing moustache and a rather prominent belly, she was an intellectual person, as interested in the arts and learning as he was. She attended the Palace School and Theodulf, the Bishop of Orleans, and one of Charles' favorite poets, wrote, "She studiously pursues the liberal arts, storing her learning in the rententive hold of her mind."

Because of all her virtues Liutgard also made a perfect mistress for the magnificent new palace at Aachen, which had taken years to build and which was the pride of the King. The palace stood high on a hill and was constructed entirely of marble which had been brought from Italy. It was designed after the manner of Charles' other Frankish vills. The great hall on the first floor is said to have measured 150 feet by 60 or 70 feet and was graced by three large semicircular alcoves. There was a library, a hall for weapons and a strong room containing stout chests in which were stored gold, silver, jewels and other precious possessions.

THE ROYAL PALACE AT AACHEN

And on the roof there stood a great bronze eagle with out-stretched wings.

Close by the palace was an immense park completely fenced in and stocked with every imaginable beast, which Charles and his friends could hunt. If one can believe the records of the time, this park even contained tigers, rhinoceroses and dragons.

Another remarkable feature of the palace at Aachen was an enormous marble swimming pool where Charles, who was an excellent swimmer, could sport with his friends. Einhard says, "Charles used to invite not only his sons to his pool, but his nobles and friends, and now and then a troupe of his retinue or bodyguard, so that a hundred or more persons sometimes bathed with him."

Attached to the palace was a building devoted entirely to government business. The Frankish kingdom was now a vast and complicated country very different from the primitive "wilderness" realm which Charles had inherited twenty-six years before. Because of Charles' conquests, his wisdom in governing, and his programs for education and the building of roads and bridges, all the lands in his realm had prospered. Travel and trade had been stimulated, and cities flourished, towns grew larger and the "fortified places" had become thriving centers of exchange. Industries had begun to appear; enterprising men were establishing workrooms where hired labor produced such articles as armor, cloth, jewelry, musical instruments. Yes, life was now different and more complicated, and in order to run the government efficiently a whole building was needed with audience chambers, council rooms and record rooms.

The palace at Aachen with its park and pool and government building was indeed an interesting place. But it was not yet complete; at the foot of the hill on which the palace stood Charles was building a great chapel. It was Byzantine and octagonal in form and was covered by a circular dome topped with a cupola roofed with sheets of lead. A two-storied colonnade ran around the interior, "adorned with gold and silver and lamps, railings and a door of solid bronze. . . ." Inside the dome was decorated with a magnificent mosaic. Pope Hadrian gave Charles much of the material and many of these ornaments.

Charles now had a private place of worship as magnificent as any he had ever seen. While in the past he had attended mass every day, he now attended services in this chapel three and four times a day.

Surrounding the palace and Charles' beautiful chapel were houses for government officials and their many assistants—clerks, palace stewards, the students and teachers of the Palace School, visitors, foreign envoys and churchmen. These houses were many in number because most of these officials had numerous assistants and families and servants of their own.

Those who helped Charles run the government were carefully chosen from districts far and wide. In this way every locality in the realm was represented, and visitors and those seeking aid or justice could always find someone who spoke his native language.

There was a Palace Chaplain, whose duty it was to attend to all matters concerning the Church. He stood close to Charles and served as one of his principal advisers. The Chancellor attended to matters related to foreign countries such as England, Spain and Denmark. The Count of the Palace served as the highest judge of the land next to Charles himself and had charge of civil administration of the realm.

Besides these three high officers there were a Palace Chamberlain, who took care of the treasury; a Seneschal, or steward, of the palace servants; and a Constable, or "count of the stables." There were also a head doorkeeper, a cup-bearer, a master falconer, several masters of the hunt and numerous gentlemen and ladies-in-waiting.

The crowded palace was always teeming with visitors. The realm was large and nobles came from everywhere. There was an endless stream of churchmen, pilgrims, tradesmen and young men who wished to study at the Palace School. Charles welcomed all scholars who wished to come to Aachen. Some of these people stayed for a few days or weeks, but others remained at the palace for many months, even years.

Because so many people were drawn to Aachen, a little town with a marketplace sprung up nearby. It was a busy place, noisy and active, for while the food and other provisions for Charles and his court were brought in trains of ox-drawn carts from his different vills, even far-distant ones, everyone else connected with the palace had to buy his own food and supplies. Peasants from miles around brought their farm produce to the marketplace at Aachen. There one could buy eggs, chickens, cheese, squealing pigs, geese, vegetables, fruits, breads and cakes, beer and wine.

It was to this marketplace also that peddlers and merchants from distant lands brought their ribbons, jewelry, holy relics, altar cloths, vestments, furs, Oriental silks and perfumes. Jugglers and minstrels attracted by the wealth also found their way to Aachen, as did thieves, robbers and beggars.

Aachen, the new Rome which Charles had built as the capital of his realm, was indeed a beautiful and lively place —the pride of all.

Charles spent the next twenty years of his life at Aachen. He and his court no longer traveled through the realm. His kingdom was now so well organized and his missi so efficient that his presence was felt everywhere, and it was no longer necessary for him to appear in person. There were no longer any wars, and so he did not have to leave his palace to lead his armies except on occasion to discipline the faithless Saxons, who were still fighting off conversion and agitating for their freedom. All other troubles were taken care of by his officers; Charles had always been able to delegate authority. Now he was able to devote a great deal of his time to the things he loved best: his family, his friends, swimming, hunting and scholarship.

Charles was extremely attached to his family, especially his children. An old record states, "He never took his meals without them whenever he was at home, and never made a journey without them; his sons would ride at his side, and his daughters would follow him while a number of his bodyguard detailed for their protection brought up the rear."

The record continues. "Strange to say although his daughters were very handsome women and Charles loved them very dearly he was never willing to marry any of them to a man of their own nation or to a foreigner, but kept them all at home until his death, saying that he could not dispense with their society." He twice strayed from this; he once betrothed his daughter Rotrud to Constantine, the son of the Empress Irene, and Bertha to the eldest son of King Offa of England. But when the time came for the marriages to take place, he broke the engagements even at the risk of war.

Charles' attitude toward his daughters seems very stern but this was not so at all. They were very beautiful, spirited young ladies and enjoyed tremendous freedom, having countless friends and admirers.

Life in Aachen was stimulating and pleasant for Charles, what with his family, a constant flow of friends, visitors from far-off lands, his chapel and his Palace School led by his beloved Alcuin.

CHARLEMAGNE

But the years were passing and Alcuin was aging. He was now sixty, a full old age for a man in those days, and he longed for retirement. He spoke of entering the monastery at Fulda, there to spend his days in prayer and meditation preparing for his death.

Alcuin had never taken sacred vows, although he had always served the Church, and Charles was distressed at the thought of such a distinguished man becoming a lowly monk. He begged him to remain at court until he could find a suitable berth for retirement. After all, Alcuin had served him not only as private teacher and Minister of Education but also as adviser on religious and political matters. How could Charles reward him?

The opening which he sought soon came. The abbot of the monastery of Tours died, and Alcuin was appointed to fill this vacancy.

For a man seeking to spend his remaining days in peace and quiet the monastery at Tours was hardly the right place. Its lands were so vast that it had twenty thousand serfs to work them, and Alcuin was busier there than he had ever been at Aachen. Besides caring for the many monks who were in his charge, he ran the monastery school and opened a scriptorium for the copying of books which was larger and finer than any other in the realm. Added to this was a new occupation; at the palace Alcuin had been able to speak to Charles and his other friends whenever he chose, but now he had to spend many hours each day writing them long letters.

140

THE ROYAL PALACE AT AACHEN

While Alcuin was plunged into a busier life than ever, he enjoyed his activity, complaining only that he missed the worldly ways of the court and feared that at Tours he was becoming a "rustic."

Now Charles could relax, happy in the knowledge that his dear friend and teacher was leading a fulfilled and contented life.

THE ROYAL PALACE AT AACHEN

15

Pope Leo III

On Christmas day, 795, Pope Hadrian died, and on the day of his burial, a new pope, Leo III, was elected. The two events followed so quickly upon each other that everyone was shocked, even Charles in far-off Aachen. It was suspected everywhere that the new pope, whose reputation was clouded with rumors of broken vows, forgery and other dishonesties, had bought his high position.

The nobles of Rome were outspoken in their opposition to

Leo, but they were not alone. The people of Rome among whom Leo had been born were also against him. And so Leo's situation was very insecure. In an attempt to fortify his shaky position he lost no time trying to win Charles over.

Leo knew that Hadrian had never humbled himself before Charles, but he needed Charles, the Patriarch of Rome, so badly that he bowed and scraped before him. He sent him the banner of the city and the symbolic keys to the Tomb of St. Peter's, vowing obedience and loyalty. To impress Charles still further he asked him to send an envoy at once to receive the oath of allegiance from the people of Rome.

These were flattering gestures indeed, but Charles apparently was not impressed. He wrote the Pope a letter which indirectly suggested that His Holiness should mend his ways. Among other things, it advised Leo henceforth "to always follow the sacred laws of the Holy Fathers" and serve as "a shining example of perfect virtue."

The envoy whom Charles sent to Rome to receive the people's oath of allegiance was also armed with advice for the Pontiff. Charles had written instructions containing such phrases as "admonish our apostolic lord to be honorable in all his conduct and especially to regard the Holy Canons" and "advise him most urgently to put a stop to the heretical sale of offices and other abuses."

It is obvious that Charles did not think too highly of the new pope, but there is no indication that he entertained the idea of removing Leo from office and of ordering the election of another pope. Under Alcuin's influence, Charles felt that, right or wrong, the high position of pope must be supported.

To protect the dignity of the Church, Charles was willing to accept Leo III regardless of his faults. Among the Roman clergy, however, there were many who felt otherwise, and they were led by two high churchmen of the Vatican, Campulus and Pashalis. Pashalis was a nephew of the late Hadrian.

The feeling in Rome against Leo grew so intense that a plot against his life soon developed. It was conceived and carried out by the aristocrats of Rome, of whom Pashalis was a member. On April 25, 799, as Pope Leo, dressed in his most elaborate vestments, was riding through the streets of Rome at the head of a religious procession, he was suddenly attacked by a band of men who had been hiding in a dark alley. There were fellow conspirators of Pashalis and Campulus, who were riding on either side of the Pope busily engaging him in conversation. Now they turned upon him, aiding the attackers who dragged the Pope from his horse, tore off his vestments and beat him until he lost consciousness. The bystanders and those in the procession, seized with terror, fled.

Having spent their fury the conspirators left the scene. Later, however, they returned to the deserted street and, picking up the half-dead Pope, carried him to the monastery of St. Erasmus where they planned to hold him prisoner.

POPE LEO III

But that very night, under the cover of darkness, the Pope's chamberlain, Albinus, managed to get into the monastery. He brought a rope along and lowered the Pope out of his prison window. Safely on the ground below, the bruised and beaten Leo fled through the dark streets of Rome to the safety of St. Peter's outside the city walls.

This is the story of the attack as it probably occurred, but the Pope gave a slightly different version. He said that the conspirators not only beat him most severely but also attempted to cut out his tongue and blind him. His friends and supporters, in order to further their cause and impress the populace of Rome, improved upon the Pope's version; they said that the conspirators had actually cut out the Pope's tongue and blinded him but that his speech and sight had been restored by a miracle.

The attack upon the Pope and his escape so agitated the people that rioting broke out in Rome. The home of the papal chamberlain, who had rescued the Pope, was broken into. The mob plundered the house, and what they could not remove they smashed with uncontrollable fury. Such was the temper of the people against Leo.

When the news of the rioting, which amounted almost to civil war, reached the Duke of Spoletum, he rushed troops to Rome. Finding the gates closed against him, he took the Pope from St. Peter's and brought him back with him to Spoletum where His Holiness would be safe from further attack.

Charles was in Paderborn, deep in the heart of Saxony,

giving his personal attention to the problems of governing those difficult people, when the news of all this violence reached him. He at once ordered that Leo should be conducted under a protective guard and with due respect to this far-distant place and brought into his presence.

Even though by tradition popes seldom left the Vatican and the journey of eight hundred miles would be long and hard, Leo was happy to undertake the trip and come under the protection of the powerful King Charles. Besides, he would now have the opportunity of presenting his case directly and perhaps persuade Charles to punish his enemies.

When Charles was a little boy of ten and Pope John came to Frankland to visit his father, Pepin the Short, he was given the honor of meeting the Pope on the road and conducting him to the palace. Now as Pope Leo approached Paderborn, Charles sent his twenty-two-year-old son Pepin, King of Italy, who happened to be in Saxony at the time, with a guard of honor to greet Leo.

In the meantime Charles ordered the nobles and clergy who were with him and his troops to assemble in a great circle outside the palace. Within this circle the clergy formed a smaller circle under the sacred banner of the cross. In the center of all stood Charles, dressed in his finest armor and wearing a golden helmet.

As Pope Leo's procession drew close, trumpets blared and the assembled host raised their spears, clashed their shields and shouted a thunderous welcome. Charles then walked forward, kneeled for a moment before the Pope, then rose

146

and embraced him. He then led the Pope past his kneeling soldiers, and Leo blessed them as the churchmen in the inner circle chanted songs of praise.

After attending mass together in the church, the King and the Pope entered the great wooden palace where a banquet was awaiting them. Sitting side by side, Pope Leo III and Charles, King of the Franks and Lombards, feasted and drank wine from golden goblets.

The Pope stayed at Paderborn for three months, during which time Charles heard every detail of his story. However, being wise and cautious, Charles during this time also gathered as much material as possible from those opposed to the Pope; emissaries traveled between Paderborn and Rome bringing full reports of the Pope's behavior and the grievances against him.

The case against the Pope seems to have been very strong, for during those three summer months a large anti-Leo faction formed within the court. These men considered the Pope's behavior a blot on the spiritual dignity of the office, and they felt Leo should be removed.

However, Alcuin, Charles' beloved teacher and adviser, felt otherwise. He wrote Charles numerous letters revealing his position. He insisted that no one had the authority to judge a pope; that the pope was a "judge who could not be judged." Therefore he advised Charles to preserve the honor of the Papacy by hushing up the scandal and to avoid, at all costs, a public trial.

There is reason to believe that Charles felt Leo was guilty,

147

but it is obvious that he also agreed with Alcuin that the dignity of the Papacy must be preserved. To depose the pope would undermine the authority of the Papacy by admitting that this highest and holiest office of the Church could be held by a man who was evil and corrupt. So he decided to support Leo against his enemies and replace him upon the throne of St. Peter.

There was one difficulty, however. The people of Rome, especially the aristocrats, were solidly against Leo, and their opinion was shared by large numbers in the rest of Italy. To restore the Pope's dignity and authority, he would have to be publicly cleansed of the charges against him; an investigation of the entire problem would have to be held in Rome. So in the fall of 799, Charles sent Leo back to Rome under a heavy guard, accompanied by two archbishops and a group of *missi* who were instructed to conduct the investigation.

Leo was not welcomed back by the people. Their feelings against him were so strong that while he remained secluded in his palace, a virtual prisoner, Pashalis and Campulus and the other conspirators enjoyed complete freedom. In fact the people and the conspirators felt their case was so strong that when the conspirators appeared before the investigating commission they added little or nothing to the accusations already presented. They assumed the verdict would be against the Pope. But they were wrong.

To save the dignity of the Church, Charles had instructed his *missi* on what the verdict should be. So the Pope was declared innocent and his accusers were arrested and sent to Frankland.

By this highhanded method Charles had hoped to settle the question once and for all, but he was soon to discover how mistaken he was. The tension in Rome only increased.

Charles hoped that time would cool the heat of anger in Rome. While waiting for this to happen he decided to go on a tour of his kingdom. He had not done this in some years, and there were many matters which demanded his attention, the most pressing of these being raids upon his Frankish coast by Norsemen.

The inhabitants of Scandinavia, who at this early date were beginning to divide into the different nations which we know today as Denmark, Norway and Sweden, began to prowl the North Sea in their longboats seeking loot and land for expansion. They had started by raiding Britain and the Frisian Islands along the coast of Saxony but were now so bold that they were raiding Charles' Channel ports and the coast of Aquitaine.

Charles visited many of the sites which had been raided, trying to decide how to combat this enemy. His experience in the past had always been on land and with armies, but now he was forced to turn toward the sea. However, this did not trouble him. He was ever flexible and ready to accept new challenges. And so, Einhard tells us that "he fitted out a fleet for war with the Norsemen; the vessels required for this purpose were built on the rivers that flow from

Gaul and Germany into the Northern Ocean." He also caused all harbors to be patrolled and watchtowers to be built along the coast "and at the mouths of rivers large enough to admit the entrance of vessels to prevent the enemy from disembarking."

However, the Norse raids were not the only attacks which Charles suffered from the sea at this period. The Moors or Mohammedans of northern Africa began pirate raids on the islands of the Mediterranean and the Mediterranean coast of Gaul and Italy. The people of the islands of Minorca and Majorca begged Charles to save them from these bloodthirsty pirates. He sent troops to defend these islands and built a Mediterranean fleet, setting up the same system of watchtowers and guards that he had in the north. "Hence," says Einhard, "Italy suffered no great harm at the hands of the Moors nor Gaul and Germany from the Norsemen."

Having taken care of these pressing matters Charles now went to visit his beloved Alcuin at Tours. As was the custom his queen, Liutgard, and his entire family and court traveled with him. It was a happy gathering, but suddenly it all turned to grief. The beautiful and loving Liutgard became ill and died, and there at Tours with Alcuin at his side Charles buried his fifth and last wife.

16

Charles, Emperor of the Romans

Charles had hoped that time would soften the anger of the Romans against Leo III, but their hatred only deepened as time went on.

Realizing that this condition could not be tolerated any longer, Charles decided to personally settle the matter for all time. Accompanied by his entire court, his daughters and his sons, Charles and Pepin, he started out for Rome in the fall of A.D. 800 at the head of a great and colorful procession.

CHARLEMAGNE

The Field of March, which was held that year in August, had granted him a large contingent of troops for this trip. Many churchmen and nobles from all parts of his realm were also with him; and all, including a long train of ox-drawn carts carrying provisions and presents for the Pope, followed him through the high, dangerous and winding passes of the Alps and down the Italian peninsula to the Holy City.

Reaching Rome, Charles immediately called together a synod, or council of Church dignitaries, to hear the charges leveled against Leo by his enemies. He had not forgotten that Alcuin had advised him against putting the Pope on trial, but the situation was such that he had no alternative.

The trial lasted for three long weeks. Pashalis, Campulus and the other conspirators whom Charles had brought from Frankland with him testified once more against the Pope. But while many refuted them and defended Leo, Charles was not able to get the verdict he wanted. While the court did not condemn Leo, it nevertheless could not clear him of the ugly charges leveled against him!

Charles was deeply embarrassed by the failure of the court to pronounce the Pope innocent, and he felt that now only one avenue lay open: the Pope would have to clear himself publicly by taking a solemn oath and declaring his innocence before God. And so on the twenty-third of December before Charles, the members of the synod and all those people of Rome who could crowd into St. Peter's, Pope Leo III swore to his innocence.

CHARLES, EMPEROR OF THE ROMANS

From the pulpit close to the sacred tomb of St. Peter his voice rang out, "Of my own free will, I, Leo, Pope of the Holy Roman Church, swear before God, who knows my conscience, and before St. Peter, Prince of the Apostles, in whose basilica we are now gathered, that I have not committed or caused to be committed the hateful crimes of which I have been accused."

As the last of the Pope's words faded into silence the great basilica filled with the sound of song. Charles and all the churchmen present raised their voices in praise to God, the Virgin Mary and the saints.

Pope Leo now stood innocent before all. The conscience of Christendom had at last been appeased.

Two days later, on Christmas day, A.D. 800, another theatrical and astonishing event took place in St. Peter's basilica.

It had been whispered about for some time that on that day a very unusual event would take place and that Charles, King of the Franks and Lombards, would leave the most holy of Christian churches in Europe a very different person from what he had been. Because of this, vast crowds packed the basilica. The Frankish, Saxon, Bavarian and Aquitainian nobles who had come with Charles to Rome mingled with a great throng of Romans, Lombards and Greeks. And all were gripped with the excitement of expectation.

In honor of this most holy day, Christmas, the basilica had been beautifully decorated. Purple curtains had been drapped between the columns of the central nave. The flickering flames of three thousand candles lighted the altar and the gold and jewel studded tomb of St. Peter. Pope Leo and his attendant priests were dressed in their most sumptuous and colorful vestments.

As the mysteries of the high mass unfolded amid the smoke of incense, the clear tinkling of altar bells, the murmur of prayers, the crossings and genuflexions and the echo of musical chantings, the throng watched Charles. Wearing the Roman toga and cloak bound with a golden belt, he was stationed near the altar flanked by his daughters and his two sons, Charles and Pepin.

With the end of the mass came the moment for which all had been waiting. As Charles rose from his knees the Pope produced a crown of gold and placed it upon his head. In that instant the whole basilica resounded with the acclamation, "To Charles Augustus, crowned of God, the great and pacific Emperor, long life and victory."

Twice more Charles was acclaimed with these stirring words. Then Pope Leo sank to his knees and humbly kissed the hem of Charles' toga while those assembled broke into song calling upon the saints to bless the new emperor, his children and all his subjects.

To add to this most unusual ceremony, the Pope now anointed young Charles, placed a crown upon his head and proclaimed him King of Western Neustria.

Pepin was King of Italy, Louis was King of Aquitaine and young Charles was King of West Neustria. Over these three kings and what remained of the realm ruled their father, Charles, the Emperor.

There can be no doubt that Pope Leo and Charles had carefully planned this coronation. Historians believe that Charles had discussed it in detail with his nobles and his advisers, especially Alcuin, the year before when he went on the tour of his realm.

All appear to have encouraged him. But Einhard seems to indicate that Charles soon regretted the step he had taken. Einhard seems to imply that the Pope led Charles on in this matter and deceived him as to the far-reaching significance of assuming the title of Emperor. Referring to this historical Christmas day of A.D. 800 Einhard says, "It was then that Charles received the titles of Emperor and Augustus, to which he first had such an aversion that he declared he would not have set foot in the church the day they were conferred, although it was a great feast day, if he could have foreseen the design of the Pope."

What was "the design of the Pope"?

The first part of the Pope's "design" is simple and obvious. As Emperor and Augustus of the Romans Charles could now try and condemn those who had conspired against the Pope and completely vindicate him, a matter which Charles attended to without delay. But the second part of his "design" was shrewd and devious, and from Einhard's statement it is clear that Charles did not comprehend its ramifications and complications. It involved a power struggle between the East and West; the Papacy was trying to free it-

155

self from the Roman emperors in Constantinople. It wanted a European Roman Empire in which the Roman Church would be supreme, and Charlemagne with his "new Rome" at Aachen was exactly what the Papacy needed. Charles was a Frank not a Latin, and Aachen was a true European capital.

In the year A.D. 330 when Constantine, the first Christian Emperor, moved the capital of the Roman Empire from Rome to the new city of Constantinople on the Bosporus, the budding Christian Church moved with him. The Church of Rome, which had been founded by St. Peter himself and where his body lay buried, was thus forced into a secondary position. However, the Bishops of Rome, who later became known by the title of Pope, never accepted this degradation. Through the centuries they firmly maintained that the Roman Church was the true Church, founded by St. Peter in fulfillment of Christ's wish.

Now, with the advent of Charles, a most pious Christian, the Roman Church had gained tremendous power in Europe, and it felt that the time had come to assert its position. Italy and the rest of Europe technically belonged under the rule of the Roman Emperor in Constantinople, but because of the great distance and shocking corruption in the palace in Constantinople, contact and control had been lost. Besides, the imperial throne was occupied by Irene, a woman so evil that in order to assume power she had not only poisoned her husband but then blinded and killed her son. The Papacy reasoned that no one could accept such a woman as ruler. But even if Irene had not been corrupt, a woman could not be Emperor of Rome. The throne was, therefore, considered vacant, and who was more devout, more Christian, more entitled to be Emperor than Charles, ruler of most of Europe?

These arguments seemed reasonable to Charles, and so he allowed the imperial crown to be pressed upon his brow. Immediately following his coronation he happily began exercising his newly assumed powers as Emperor upon the people of Rome.

He had the Pope and the people of Rome swear an oath of allegiance to him. He imposed taxes upon them, put them under the supervision of his *missi,* issued decrees and imperial coins, and required that all documents should henceforth be dated by the years of his reign. And to make sure that no pope could ever again be elected so quickly after the death of a previous pope, he made it a law that a new pope could only assume power with his, the Emperor's, written consent. In short, no pope could in the future ascend the throne of St. Peter without Charles' permission.

Having settled his affairs in Rome, Charles started back toward Aachen shortly after Easter in the year 801. But he was no longer as happy and relaxed as he had been, for reports had reached him concerning Constantinople's reaction to his acceptance of the title of Emperor—a reaction which Charles had apparently not foreseen.

Constantinople, it seemed, was extremely displeased. It protested that Charles was an impostor, and it warned that there could be only one Roman Emperor, the Emperor in Constantinople.

Mulling over these reports Charlemagne was filled with anxiety. Would it mean war? War with the Eastern Empire was something he must avoid at all costs. But how could he do so?

He sent many emissaries and letters to Constantinople in an attempt to heal the breach and for a long time avoided using his title. But it did not help. Then suddenly a solution presented itself. In order to still Constantinople's anger and tie the hands of the Empress Irene, Charles reached a fantastic decision. Why should not the two Christian Empires be joined as one? Why should not he and Irene marry? He was fifty-eight and she was fifty. Besides, she was reputed to be the most beautiful woman in the world.

Intoxicated with his plan, Charles immediately dispatched ambassadors to Constantinople to ask for her hand, and Irene, who had rejected all men since that day long ago when she had poisoned her husband and lived entirely surrounded by crafty eunuchs, surprisingly accepted. Exactly why she did this no one knows.

However, this dramatic, if not fantastic, scheme did not come about. The marriage which was to join the Eastern Roman Empire and the Western Roman Empire never took place because, while Irene was willing to marry Charlemagne, no one else in her court approved. They were so set against having a foreign master that a palace plot developed.

Irene was overthrown and a general named Nicephorus mounted the throne.

Thus ended the reign of Irene the Empress. But it is not the last that history records of her. She was sent into exile on the ancient Isle of Lesbos, where she was forced to support herself by spinning and where she died the following year. Her body was then brought back to Constantinople, and she was hailed as a martyr and canonized in the Greek Church as St. Irene. This came about because of popular demand. Despite the fact that she was known to be over-zealous and personally ambitious, the multitudes loved her because she was beautiful and had always cast gold coins among them as she rode by!

17

Providing for the Future

The death of the Empress Irene destroyed Charlemagne's dream of uniting the two great Christian empires and thus avoiding war. He did not, however, give up his efforts to maintain peace and soon devised another plan.

In the year 799 while Charlemagne was in Aachen, and again two days before his coronation in Rome in the year 800, he had received ambassadors from the Patriarch of Jerusalem expressing their lord's admiration and friendship and bearing gifts. The first time these emissaries had brought holy relics and the second time the banner of Jerusalem and the symbolic keys of the Holy Sepulcher.

Later Charlemagne had received ambassadors of friendship from the Caliph Harun al Rashid of Baghdad ruler of the great Moslem Empire, and so he reasoned, "With such friends as these in the Moslem world would Constantinople dare to make war against me?" He thought not. Besides, he knew that there was great animosity between Constantinople and Baghdad. The Emperor Nicephorus, Irene's successor, was very aggressive and arrogant toward the Mohammedan world, and war was threatening. Since Harun al Rashid and his people were obviously the stronger of the two it was good diplomacy for Charles to court his favor. Was it not better to have an infidel as one's friend than to run the risk of being overrun by a Christian enemy? So Charles furthered his friendship with Harun al Rashid. A constant flow of emissaries traveled the long road back and forth between Aachen and Baghdad, carrying messages filled with compliments and goodwill and bearing gifts.

Charlemagne's empire was, by comparison, a very primitive one; the people of Europe were still mired in the ignorance and crudities of their barbarian past. While they had a few fine things such as furs, woolen cloth and capes and beautifully wrought jewelry, most of Charles' gifts to the Caliph were rather simple. Harun al Rashid, on the other hand, sent Charles the most magnificent silks, brocades, books, spices, perfumes, rare glass and ornamental brasses.

161

CHARLEMAGNE

The nations that made up his empire included some of the most civilized people in the world. They had universities, great public libraries, and they were highly advanced in agriculture, astronomy, philosophy, mathematics and medicine. They produced the very first books on medicine which correctly diagnosed many illnesses such as smallpox and measles. They were the first in the Middle Ages to have apothecary schools, apothecary shops and dispensaries. They used animal gut in sutures and inhalation of certain drugs to produce anesthesia.

While the cities of Europe were little more than large towns, dark and squalid, the Moslem Empire could boast of magnificent metropolises with beautiful buildings, parks and paved streets which were lighted at night and patrolled by police.

Two of the most wondrous gifts that Harun al Rashid sent Charles were a brass water-clock and a tent.

Clocks were unknown in Europe at this time; there were only sundials and hourglasses. The clock which Harun al Rashid sent struck the hours by dropping brass balls into a bowl and was ornamented with twelve windows out of which at the proper moment emerged twelve miniature knights dressed in full armor and mounted on horses! The tent was so large and divided into so many rooms that people said it was as big as a palace.

These two gifts were the marvel of the time, but there was still another gift more wonderful than these. It was an elephant!

PROVIDING FOR THE FUTURE

There had not been an elephant in Europe since Hannibal, a thousand years before, had landed in Spain, marched across southern Gaul and crossed the Alps, invading the Italian peninsula. Charles had read about elephants in bestiaries, and through emissaries he had asked his friend Harun al Rashid to send him one. Two of his emissaries died en route, but one, Isaac, alone and unaided, managed to bring the great beast back.

Isaac and Abul Abbas, for that was the elephant's name, were held up in Italy for several months because Isaac did not dare to cross the Alps in midwinter as Hannibal had done. He feared that the beast might slip on the narrow icy passes or sink hopelessly into the deep snow.

In the spring, however, Isaac and his charge got through and headed north for Aachen. The word of their progress went before them, and people came from miles about to gape and stare.

When Isaac and Abul Abbas reached Aachen the members of the court also gaped and stared. Even Charlemagne could barely believe what he beheld, and Abul Abbas immediately won his heart. From that time on he took Abul Abbas with him wherever he went.

While holding Constantinople at bay through his friendship with the Caliph Harun al Rashid, and while leaving the border skirmishes and other minor military operations to his sons and generals, Charlemagne devoted himself to improving his government and his laws. Being a very pious person he had always believed that after death he would have to account to God for his conduct as a man and ruler. And so now, in the evening years of his life, he tried to improve the state of his realm.

For some years past, Charlemagne had heard rumors about corruption among his *missi,* and so he now reorganized this government service. He had formerly appointed many poor men as *missi,* but he decided henceforth to use only wealthy men so that they could not be tempted by bribes.

At this time, too, Charlemagne enacted strict new laws forbidding anyone from taking advantage of widows, orphans and foreigners. Powerful people such as counts and bishops were especially warned not to oppress the weak. Bishops, abbots and abbotesses must not oppress those under their rule; they must govern with love, charity and mercy. They must also abide strictly by their vows and avoid traveling about, drunkenness and all other forms of carousing. Charles' previous warnings on these matters had apparently not taken effect.

Judges must render honest verdicts according to the law and not according to their personal feelings. Murder now became a crime against the state. Until this time murder had been looked upon in the ancient Germanic tribal way, as a minor offense; theft was punishable by death but murder by only a trifling fine. Now, even though murder was still not punishable by death, it was looked upon from the Christian viewpoint, as a highly immoral act.

So many men had become priests and entered monasteries in order to avoid serving in the army that Charlemagne now effected military reforms. Henceforth no one could become a priest without his permission. He also revised the conscription laws so that only those able to pay a tax could escape service.

Charles ordered that no one in his entire land should refuse pilgrims food and lodging. And he revised the oath which his subjects were required to take. Since he, the Emperor, could not personally supervise the conduct of each man, woman and child, he had his subjects swear that they would lead good Christian lives, being honest and God-fearing at all times.

These were some of the many reforms which Charlemagne instituted after becoming Emperor, but the most significant of all concerned the codification of all the laws of the different peoples who made up his empire. Each group lived under its own laws, and in order to clarify these laws and make it easier to dispense justice, Charles now ordered that they be written down and clearly defined.

When Charles was not occupied with his reforms he spent his time among the scholars at his court and in his favorite sports, swimming and hunting. It was a pleasant and satisfying life, but suddenly in 804 the obstinate and unruly Saxons once more rose up in revolt. Charles was again forced onto the field of battle.

Leading an army he left Aachen, crossed the Rhine and entered Saxony. He took with him his pride and joy, Abul Abbas, his great and wondrous elephant. After only a few short months he put down the rebellion and started back for home, bringing with him a vast horde of Saxon men, women and children, to be scattered far and wide over his empire.

This was the last mass deportation of Saxons. By now so many of them had been deported from Saxony that further resistance was impossible, and so the long war against the Saxons, a war which had lasted, off and on, for thirty-two out of Charlemagne's sixty-two years, was now over.

However, this final revolt of the Saxons was not the only problem that preyed upon Charles' mind at this period. Just before leaving on his campaign against the Saxons, he had received the news of the death, at Tours, of his beloved teacher Alcuin, who had been struck down by a paralytic stroke. It was a loss which moved Charles deeply and which created a void in his life.

Returning now from Saxony he was faced with skirmishes with the Slavs on his northeastern frontier, Arab pirate attacks on his Aquitainian ports and war with Constantinople.

Charlemagne was not directly involved in any of the fighting. Young Charles led the army against the Slavs, Louis took care of the Arabs and Pepin fought Constantinople, yet it was a very worrying time. It was made more so because no decisive victory could be won against the Slavs and Arabs. The barbaric Slavs were to continue to harry the northeastern frontier for many many years, and the problem with the Arab pirates was not settled for over a thousand years, or until 1830 when the French conquered Algiers. The trouble with Constantinople was the only one of these three problems to be decided at this time, but even that was not too satisfactory.

Through diplomatic moves Charles had gained control for Pepin's Lombard kingdom of Venetia and Dalmatia, two provinces on the Adriatic which belonged to the Byzantine Empire. Constantinople naturally resented this seizure and sent a fleet to blockade the city of Venice, which was at that time only beginning to rise in power.

Venice, taking fright, immediately returned her allegiance to Constantinople, but Charles was not to be put off. He ordered Pepin to take his Mediterranean fleet and drive off the blockading vessels. In the naval encounter which ensued, Charles' fleet was vanquished and had to withdraw. But Constantinople did not pursue its advantage. And Charles, submitting to the situation, quietly dropped his claims to Dalmatia and did not look for any more engagements.

It was obvious that neither Charlemagne nor the Emperor Nicephorus wanted to become involved in a full-scale war. In fact, history records that Charles only wanted to aggravate the Emperor and prove to him that he had power on sea as well as on land. He wanted to prove to Nicephorus that he was his equal if not his superior and that Nicephorus would do well to become his friend and recognize him as Emperor of the Romans in the West.

This triple set of troubles brought clearly into focus for the aging Charles the need for his three sons to work together and rule as one after his death. He remembered only too clearly how after his father's death the Frankish kingdom had been torn asunder and dangerously weakened by the animosity which existed between him and his brother Carloman, and he did not want this to happen to his empire.

Charlemagne, therefore, drew up a document legally dividing his realm into the three kingdoms which he had already given to Charles, Pepin and Louis and augmenting each by the lands which bordered upon them. Louis got Aquitaine, the southern part of Burgundy and the Spanish March. Pepin got Lombardy, part of Alemannia and Bavaria. And Charles got everything else including Saxony—he got the largest part.

This document also included definite rules of conduct for his sons to follow in preserving the unity of the empire. Young Charles, Pepin and Louis were instructed to live forever at peace with one another; never to plot against each other or invade each other's territories; to help each other against all internal and external enemies. They were always to support the Roman Church and join together and act as one in its defense. While any freeman could travel freely between the three kingdoms, no brother was to harbor a criminal who escaped from another brother's kingdom. Marriages between the people of the three kingdoms were to be encouraged because they would help bind the people together. If one of the brothers should die his kingdom was to be divided between the remaining brothers unless he had a son whom he wanted to inherit it.

Charlemagne ended this document with a plea for his grandsons born or yet to be born. He knew how cruel men could be, and while he trusted his sons, nevertheless he wanted to provide against all contingencies. He said, "We order that none of our sons, for any reason whatsoever, shall have any of our grandsons . . . put to death, mutilated, blinded or forcibly tonsured without a fair trial. . . . On the contrary, we wish them to be held in honor by their fathers and uncles."

To impress upon all how deeply and earnestly he wished these provisions to be followed, Charlemagne now took an extraordinary step. He, the Emperor, a man who had never taken orders from a pope, sent the document to Rome to have it witnessed and signed by Leo III.

18

A Ball of Fire

Charlemagne thought that by drawing up a document legally dividing his realm and having it signed by the Pope, the future would be assured. But he was wrong. He could not foresee what lay ahead, and in a very few years uncontrollable events made useless all his careful provisions.

In 808, just four years after the drawing up of this historic paper, Charlemagne's kingdom was suddenly attacked by the Norsemen. The Danes, under King Gottrik, raided the northern borders of Saxony. Being repulsed they withdrew and during the following year worked without rest building a great earthen embankment across the neck of their peninsula from the North Sea to the Baltic. This wall had only one opening, a narrow door through which merchants could pass to and fro between Saxony and Denmark.

The Danes felt secure behind their great wall and now launched an attack by two hundred ships on the Frisian Islands and coastal towns.

This raiding flotilla of long, black boats with their high prows carved like dragons or great serpents, square sails of brightly colored stripes and robber sea warriors crouching behind round painted shields swept down with terrifying swiftness upon the Frisians. They killed the people, burned their homes and farms and then quickly withdrew, carrying with them what spoils they had gathered.

From the reports which Charlemagne received, he knew that this raid was only the opening attack of an extensive campaign against him. Einhard reports, "King Gottrik was so puffed with vain aspirations that he intended conquering all the Germanic peoples, and looked upon Saxony and Frisia as his provinces. . . . He . . . boasted that he would shortly appear with a great army before Aachen." And so although Charlemagne was now sixty-eight, a very advanced age for a man at that period, he would not allow the threat to go unchallenged and decided personally to lead an army against the Danes.

Crossing the Rhine with a small force, he entered Saxony.

171

There he halted to await the arrival of the rest of his army. And it was at this time that the first of a series of misfortunes occurred which, with mounting intensity, were to harass him to the end of his life. Abul Abbas his wonderful elephant suddenly died.

Charlemagne grieved for Abul Abbas as though he had lost a friend, and the news, spreading quickly through the realm, filled all who heard it with forebodings. They felt that it was a bad omen. Their fears were confirmed only a few weeks later when Charlemagne, who had now advanced as far north as Verden, received the news that his eldest daughter by Hildegarde, his lovely Rotrud, had died—Rotrud, his beautiful blond-haired daughter who had been a member of the Academy and whom many years before he had betrothed to the Empress Irene's son Constantine.

Charlemagne was so crushed that he had little desire to continue the game of war, and things might have gone badly with him had not fate intervened. A plot against Gottrik developed in Denmark; there were many who were against waging war with the powerful Charlemagne. They said that Gottrik's wall was of little protection and that the Danes would surely be wiped out. And so, as history records, Gottrik was murdered by one of his own bodyguard, and the war suddenly ended.

This was a stroke of good fortune, but it was the only good fortune Charlemagne had that year. A plague which had begun in southern Italy was now sweeping through his realm. Before leaving Verden he received the tragic news that his thirty-three-year-old son Pepin, King of Italy, was dead, leaving a son, Bernard, and five daughters.

The entire atmosphere was charged with disaster. Added to the plague which was killing thousands in his empire, a pestilence now broke out among the cattle all over Europe. The oxen and other beasts which Charlemagne had with his army in Saxony were wiped out, depriving his forces of food and transportation.

Before he could leave Verden and return to Aachen, another dark happening occurred. Einhard records,

> Charles saw a ball of fire fall from the heaven with a great light, just as he was leaving camp before sunrise. . . . It rushed across the sky from right to left, and everybody was wondering what was the meaning of the sign, when the horse which Charles was riding gave a sudden plunge, head foremost, and fell, and threw him to the ground so heavily that his cloak buckle was broken and his sword-belt broken; and after his servants had hastened to him and relieved him of his arms, he could not rise without their assistance. He happened to have a javelin in his hand when he was thrown, and this was struck from his grasp with such force that it was found lying a distance of twenty feet or more from the spot.

Returning to Aachen, the darkness and ill fortune which had surrounded Charlemagne lifted for a brief time. Ambassadors were awaiting him from the Emperor Nicephorus, who had finally reached the decision that he could not continue with two powerful enemies on his borders, Harun al Rashid's Moslem Empire and Charlemagne's Western Roman Empire.

The envoys said that Emperor Nicephorus was willing to recognize Charlemagne's title of Emperor of the Romans and that he wished to express his love and friendship for his Christian brother. It was his desire that their two empires should prosper and live in peace forevermore.

Thus it was that a peace treaty was signed between the two emperors. Thus it was that the long years which Charlemagne had spent cultivating the friendship of Harun al Rashid finally bore fruit. Thus it was that two Roman Empires were recognized, the Eastern Roman, or Byzantine Empire, and the Western Roman Empire.

The settlement of his difficulties with the Emperor Nicephorus was welcome indeed but still Charlemagne could not forget the series of tragedies which had occurred while he was in Saxony. Neither could he forget the ball of fire which had fallen from the sky. He felt that it had some ominous significance. He was an excellent horseman and had never been thrown before. This accident, following so closely upon the deaths of Rotrud, Pepin and his elephant, together with the plague and the pestilence, unnerved him. He felt that there was some mysterious evil force surrounding him and that his death was approaching.

Not only Charlemagne but everyone else at court felt this was so, because during the last few years there had been numerous other evil omens. A firsthand account says:

> Eclipses of both the sun and the moon were very
> frequent . . . and a black spot was visible on the sun
> for a space of seven days. The gallery between the
> basilica and the palace which Charles had built with
> great pains and labor fell in suddenly to the ground on
> the day of the Ascension of our Lord. The wooden bridge
> over the Rhine at Mayence [Metz] which he had caused
> to be constructed with admirable skill at the cost of
> ten years hard work, so that it seemed that it might last
> forever, was so completely consumed in three hours by
> an accidental fire that not a single splinter of it was
> left except what was under the water. . . . The palace
> at Aachen frequently trembled, the roofs of whatever
> buildings he tarried in kept up a continuing crackling
> noise, the basilica . . . was struck by lightning and
> the gilded ball that adorned the pinnacle was shattered
> by the thunderbolt.

Death was surely approaching, and so Charlemagne, who
was now seventy years old, began to prepare for the salvation of his soul. Besides attending religious services three
times each day as he had done ever since his chapel at
Aachen was completed, he now also spent long hours in
prayer and in reading holy writings. He even contemplated
giving up his crown and entering a monastery or taking up
the pilgrim's staff and visiting the many holy shrines in his
realm. However, since it was not quite possible for him to

throw aside his obligations as ruler, he decided instead to do penance for his sins by wearing a hair shirt under his regular Frankish dress.

At this time also he made his will. It was signed by thirty of his most faithful friends and stipulated that all his wealth "in gold, silver, precious stones and royal ornaments" should be divided into "three lots." Two of these lots should then be divided into twenty-one parts and placed in twenty-one boxes and given to the archbishops of the twenty-one great cities of his land. The third lot was to be divided into four parts. The first part was to be shared by the twenty-one great cities, the second part was to be distributed as alms for the poor throughout his land, the third was to be given to his palace servants, and the fourth, a mere twelfth of his treasure, was to be divided among his children and his grandchildren.

Charlemagne left further instructions that the books which he had collected in his library in great numbers should be sold for fair prices and the money given to the poor.

He also directed that "the square silver table upon which there is a representation of the city of Constantinople should be sent to the Basilica of St. Peter the Apostle at Rome." A round silver table "with the representation of the city of Rome shall be given to the church at Ravenna." A third silver table which surpassed "the other two in weight and beauty of workmanship and is made in three circles, showing the plan of the whole universe . . . shall go" together with "a large and massive golden table to his heirs and to alms."

Charlemagne was now ready for death. But his days were not yet to end, and he was to suffer two more great sorrows.

During the year 811 he received the news that his first-born son, Pepin the Hunchback, had died at the monastery in Prum. Charlemagne had long ago forgiven Pepin for his part in the plot against his life, and he was as deeply hurt by this loss as by the death of Rotrud and Pepin, King of Italy. Then before his grief had lifted, on the fourth of December of that same year, 811, he lost his favorite son, young Charles.

Now of all his three heirs only Louis, King of Aquitaine, the weakest and least capable of his sons, remained.

Weighed down by grief Charlemagne now turned more and more toward religion.

He spent his days writing messages to the people of his realm, messages which were read by heralds in every city, town and hamlet of his vast empire. He reminded his people of their duties as Christians. He asked them to put envy and hatred aside and to love one another. He reminded them that life was short and that goodness was rewarded and evil punished through all eternity. He advised them to do penance for their sins while there was still time and to be merciful to all and give alms to the poor.

At this time, also, Charlemagne exchanged many long letters with high churchmen—bishops and archbishops—concerning all sorts of church matters. He made plans to hold a series of Church councils in different parts of his realm, and together with some Greek scholars he began correcting the Latin text of the Four Gospels which St. Jerome had translated from the Greek late in the fourth century.

Charlemagne would have liked to withdraw completely from public life and devote his last days to the service of God. But the problem of his succession had to be settled. All his carefully thought out plans for the succession were now rendered useless, and he was much disturbed that there remained only two possible heirs, his weak son Louis and his grandson, little Bernard, son of the late Pepin, King of Italy.

There were many at court who tried to influence Charlemagne to disinherit Louis and give the crown to Bernard. However, there was another faction, headed by Einhard, which strongly supported Louis. Charlemagne seems to have wavered between both groups, but finally reached a decision. He pronounced Bernard King of Italy and rightful successor to his father Pepin, at the same time making it clear that Louis would become Emperor. This meant that Louis would inherit the whole realm and that Bernard would be subservient to him.

Having made his intention clear Charlemagne spent the next few months instructing Louis on how to rule. He thought that he might, even now, at this last moment, be able to instill in his weak son the strength and courage necessary to all rulers. Louis, who was thirty-two years old, had become King of Aquitaine when he was only three.

A BALL OF FIRE

He had ruled his kingdom for twenty-nine years, but during that time Charlemagne had been forced to come to his help on many occasions.

Charlemagne told Louis always to love God and abide by the Ten Commandments. He instructed him on how to be the protector of the Church while ruling it with a strong hand, as he had always done. He warned him to use only honest and God-fearing men to represent him as *missi*, to love and honor all priests and to protect the poor at all times. And he tried to impress upon Louis his fervent wish that he should always show the utmost kindness to his sisters, his nephew and all his other relatives—a wish which fell upon deaf ears, for very shortly after Charlemagne was dead, Louis sent his fun-loving sisters to nunneries and had his nephew Bernard, King of Italy, blinded!

In September when Charlemagne felt that he had imparted as much wisdom of ruling as he could to Louis, he called a general assembly and proposed that his son now be acclaimed Emperor. There were many who were against this, but seeing their aged Emperor standing before them with his only son beside him they could not withhold their consent. And so on Sunday, September 11, 813, Louis was formally crowned.

The ceremony took place at the basilica at Aachen. Charlemagne, dressed in his imperial robes, which he rarely wore, robes made of cloth of gold and studded with precious stones, officiated. After prayers and a solemn sermon he placed a gold crown upon Louis' head. By doing so he made clear to all that the title of Emperor was passing from him to his son.

Then raising his voice in praise he said, "Blessed be Thou, O Lord God, Who hast granted me the grace to see with my own eyes my son seated on my throne!"

A contemporary account tells us, "After sending his son back to Aquitaine, although weak from age, Charles set out to hunt as usual, near his palace at Aachen, and spent the rest of the autumn in the chase." About the first of November, as winter was setting in, he returned to the palace where he took up once more his revisions of the Gospels.

On the twenty-second of January he was suddenly stricken with a high fever and took to his bed. From the record of his symptoms it is believed that he had an infection of the lungs and pleurisy. But he did not like doctors, and so "he prescribed for himself abstinence from food . . . thinking that the disease could be driven off, or at least mitigated, by fasting."

He died at nine o'clock on the morning of January 28, 814, after partaking of the Holy Communion. He was seventy-one years old.

There was some question as to where to bury him. Some felt that he should be buried at St. Denis next to his grandfather, Charles the Hammer, his father, Pepin the Short, and his mother, Bertrada. "But," according to Einhard, "all agreed that he could nowhere be more honorably entombed than in the very basilica that he had built at

Aachen. . . . He was buried there the same day that he died and a gilded arch was erected over his tomb."

Charlemagne's image and an inscription were engraved on this arch. The words read, "In this tomb lies the body of Charles, the Great and Orthodox Emperor who gloriously extended the kingdom of the Franks and reigned prosperously of 46 years. . . ."

Even before Charlemagne died his deeds had given rise to legends, and in the centuries that followed the stories about him increased in all parts of Europe. He was credited with feats of surpassing courage and of performing miracles.

In Germany he took on some of the aspects of the gods of Valhalla; on stormy nights he could be heard riding past on the wind, and it was his custom on clear summer nights to travel to and fro across the sky on the Milky Way in Thor's chariot. Another legend claimed that he had risen out of his grave to lead the first Crusade. He was hailed as one of the Nine Worthies. There are three Pagan Worthies: Hector, Alexander the Great and Julius Caesar; three Hebrew Worthies: Joshua, King David and Judas Maccabaeus; three Christian Worthies: King Arthur, Charlemagne and Godfrey of Bouillon.

Charlemagne was so beloved by the people of Europe that their devotion continues to this very day. Both Germans and French vie with each other claiming him as theirs, but he was neither German nor French. He was a Frank and he belonged to all Europe and to the Church. Under his rule Europe came closer to being united than it

CHARLEMAGNE

has ever been since. Under his rule paganism was eradicated
from Europe and the Christian Church firmly established.

In recognition of the great work which Charlemagne did
for the Church, he was eventually canonized. On December 2, 1162, at a great ceremony in Aachen, Charlemagne
was officially proclaimed St. Charles.

Bibliography

Ault, Warren O. *Europe in the Middle Ages*. Boston: D. C. Heath & Co., 1932.

Crombie, A. C. *Medieval and Early Modern Science*. Vol 1: *Science in the Middle Ages*. Garden City: Doubleday & Co., 1952.

Davis, H. W. Carless. *Charlemagne—Charles the Great*. New York: G. P. Putnam's Sons, 1899.

Einhard. *The Life of Charlemagne*. Ann Arbor: University of Michigan—Ann Arbor Books, 1960. (Earliest account, probably written between A.D. 817 and 830.)

Mills, Dorothy. *The Middle Ages*. New York: G. P. Putnam's Sons, 1935.

Pirenne, Henri. *Economic and Social History of Medieval Europe*. New York: Harcourt, Brace & Co., 1956.

———. *Medieval Cities*. Garden City: Doubleday & Co., 1956.

BIBLIOGRAPHY

————. *Mohammed and Charlemagne*. New York: Barnes and Noble, 1940.

Power, Eileen. *Medieval People*. New York: Barnes and Noble, 1963.

Winston, Richard. *Charlemagne, From the Hammer to the Cross*. Indianapolis: The Bobbs-Merrill Co., 1954. (Most modern and scholarly biography of Charlemagne.)

Index

185

INDEX

Bremen, 100
bridge building, 57
Britain, 15, 149
British Isles, 113
Burgundy, 16, 75, 168
Byzantine Empire, 19, 113, 158, 167, 174

Campulus, 144, 148
capitularies, 27, 83, 104-05
Capua, 109
Carloman (brother), 15-16, 22, 26-27, 28, 31
Carloman (son), 76, 86. *See also* Pepin (son)
Caroline Books, the, 124
Carolus, 26
Cathedral School of York, 92
Central Asia, 116
Channel, the, 17
Charlemagne, escorts Pope, 11-14; is brought up in religious home, 12; his family, 15; receives title of Patriarch of Rome, 16; his grandfather, 18; in battle during childhood, 19; helps conquer Aquitaine, 21; death of father, 22; is to rule with his brother, 22; description of, 23-25; his education, 25-26; open hostility between him and brother, 26-27; his capitulary on Aquitaine, 27; his first wife and their children, 28; second marriage, 30; divorce and remarriage, 30;

other children, 31, 39, 42, 68, 76, 80, 88, 101, 139; death of brother, 31-32; is King of Frankland, 32; is most powerful ruler in Europe, 33; will not take orders from Pope, 34; conquest of Saxons, 38-39; his Lombardy campaign, 41-43, 49; in Rome, 45-49; institutes "self-rule" in Lombardy, 50; death of daughter Adalhaid, 51; his royal residences, 52-55; is conscientious ruler, 56; his road and bridge building programs, 57; in all-out war against Saxons, 64-67, 70-71; relieves conditions in Lombardy, 70; his program in Saxony, 71-72; is unsuccessful in Spain, 76-78; puts down new rebellions, 81-82; introduces new laws, 83-85; death of son Lothar, 85; his plans concerning his sons' future, 86-87; refuses to give Pope lands, 90; his love for learning, 91-98; in Saxony again, 100-01, 102-04; death of wife and mother, 101; remarries, 103; his Capitulary on Saxony, 105; strikes at Beneventum, 108-09; and Tassilo, 110-12; his plan for a new Rome, 115-16; at war with the Avars, 116-19, 125-27; his treatment of the Saxons, 120; deals with

186

INDEX

heresy, 121-25; is called Charles the Great, 127; plot against his life, 128-31; death of Fastrada, 133; his fifth marriage, 134; life at Aachen, 134-39; devotion to his children, 139; and Leo III, 143-49, 151-53; builds fleets, 149-50; death of Liutgard, 150; is acclaimed Emperor, 154-57; tries to heal breach with Constantinople, 158; his friendship with Harun al Rashid, 161-63, 174; improves his government and laws, 164-65; in final revolt of Saxons, 165-66; his fleet vanquished, 167; his document dividing his realm, 168-69; is attacked by Norsemen, 171-72; death of his other children, 172, 173, 177; signs peace treaty with Constantinople, 174; feels mysterious force, 174-75; prepares for salvation of his soul, 175-76; makes his will, 176; turns more and more toward religion, 177; settles problem of his successor, 178; has his son Louis crowned Emperor, 179-80; death, 180; burial, 180-81; is canonized, 182

Charles (son), 39, 42, 68, 86, 102, 114, 151, 154, 166, 168, 177

Charles the Great. *See* Charlemagne

Charles the Hammer (grandfather), 18, 22, 74

Chasseneuil, palace at, 75

Christianity, 15, 19, 36, 63-65, 74, 82, 96, 120

Christians, 15, 18, 35, 58, 67, 74, 76

Church, the, 56-58, 59-60, 83-84, 96, 105, 119, 123, 125, 144, 156, 181-82

City of God, The, 95-96

Coliseum, the, 48

Cologne, 115

Constantine (son of Empress Irene), 107, 139, 156

Constantine the Great, 19, 89, 156

Constantinople, 13, 19, 21, 25, 42, 47, 89, 106, 116-17, 156, 157-59, 161, 166-67

Cordova, Caliph of, 74, 77

Corsica, island of, 49

Council of Frankfurt, 123-24

Council of Nicaea, 123

Dalmatia, 167

Danes. *See* Denmark

Danube River, 117, 119, 121

Denmark, 64, 72, 82, 137, 149, 170-72

Desiderata (wife), 28-30, 49

"Divine Right," rule by, 16

"Donation of Constantine," 89

INDEX

"Donation of Pepin," 21, 34, 40, 48-49
Duren, 64

Eastern Roman Empire, 19, 158, 174
Ebro River, 76
Elbe River, 103
England, 17, 36, 62, 83, 92, 137
Eresburg, fortress of, 64, 70, 71
Eric, Duke of Friuli, 125
Europe, 14, 16, 17, 18-19, 21, 22, 33, 57, 61, 92, 94, 97, 113, 156, 161, 162, 163, 173, 181-82

Fardulf, 131, 132
Fastrada (wife), 103, 104, 110, 119, 130, 133-34
Field of March, the, 14-15, 36, 64, 71, 112, 152
Flanders, 61
Florence, Italy, 108
Forum, the, 48
France, northern, 16, 22
Francia, 16
Frankfurt, 123
Frankland/Franks, 11-12, 14, description of, 16-18; 21, 22, 28, 32-33, military service in, 37; 39, life in, 52-62; 82, new laws introduced in, 83-85; 91-98, 104, 110, 112, 115, 125-126, 128, prospers under Charlemagne, 135; 149
Freya, 35

Frisian Islands, 61, 149, 171

Gascons, the, 77-78
Gaul, 17, 18, 21, 61, 149
Geneva, 40
Germans/Germany, 13, 14, 15, 27, 43, 113, 149, 164
Gisla (daughter), 88
Goths, the, 16, 75
Gottrik, King, 170-72
Graben, 121
Great St. Bernard Pass, the, 40
Greek Church, the, 159

Hadrian I, 34-35, 40, 43, 45-46, 48-49, 67, 68, 70, 85-87, 88-90, 106-10, 115, 122, 126, 136, 142
Hannibal, 163
Harun al Rashid, Caliph of Baghdad, 161-63, 174
Hela, 35
Heristal, palace at, 39
Hesse, 36
Hessi, 65
Hildegarde (daughter), 101
Hildegarde (wife), 30-31, 39, 45, 68, 75-76, 80, 88, 101-02
"Hill of Slaughter," 103
Himiltrude (wife), 28
Holland, southern part of, 16
Hungary, 16, 117
Huns, the, 16

Isle of Lesbos, 159
Ireland, 62

188

INDEX

Irene, Empress, 106-07, 116, 123, 124, 139, 156, 158-59
Irminsul, the, 38-39
Istria, 49
Italy, 13, 14, 17, 19, 29, 42, 48-49, 61, 86, 89, 92, 96, 113, 116, 150, 156, 172

James, the Apostle, 75
Jerusalem, 61, 160-61
Jordan, the, 61
Justinian, Emperor, 116

Leo III, 142-49, 151-55, 157, 169
Liege, 115
Life of Charlemagne, The, 23
Liutgard (wife), 134, 149
Liutperga, Princess, 28, 112
Lombards/Lombardy, 13-15, 19-20, 32, 41-43, 48-50, 68-70, 75, 129, 167, 168
Lombards, King of the, 13, 20, 28, 29, 31, 33-34, 40-41, 49
London, 17
Lothar (son), 80, 85
Louis (son), 80, 86-88, 114-15, 119, 154, 168, 177-80
Lyons, 125

Main River, 121
Majorca, island of, 150
medicine, 96, 162
Mediterranean, the, 18, 113, 150
Metz, 96, 102
Minorca, island of, 150

missi, 84-85, 148, 164
Mohammedans, 73-77, 150
monetary system, 83
Mongolians, 107, 110, 116
Moselle River, 39
Moslem Empire, 161-63
Mount Cenis, pass of, 41
Mount Jupiter, pass of, 40
music, 25, 96

Nantes, 21
Nero's Circus, 46
Neustria, 16, 75
Nicephorus, Emperor, 159, 161, 167, 173-74
nobles, 22, 36, 58, 84, 92, 93, 95, 129-30, 153
Norsemen, 149, 170-72
North Sea, 121, 149, 171
Norway, 149
Noyons, 22

Offa, King of England, 126, 139
Oliver, 78
Orient, the, 61, 62
Orleans, 87

Paderborn, 71, 73, 145-47
paganism, 60, 123, 124
Palace School, the, 91-93, 134, 137
Pamplona, Spain, 76
Papacy, the, 13, 20, 29, 34, 40, 43, 48, 89, 147-48, 155-56. *See also* Rome
Paris, 12, 17, 82

INDEX

Pashalis, 144, 148
Patriarch of Rome, 16
Paul the Deacon, 91, 97
Paulinus, 91
Pavia, Lombardy, 41-43, 45, 49
peasants, 58-61
Pepin (son), 87, 114, 118, 126-27, 146, 151, 154, 167, 168, 173. *See also* Carloman (son)
Pepin the Hunchback (son), 28, 31, 67, 86-87, 130-32, 177
Pepin the Short (father), 11, 13-16, 19-22, 25, 28, 74, 84, 88, 101
Persia, 18
Peter of Pisa, 91
Ponthion, 12, 14
Pope Hadrian I. *See* Hadrian I
Pope Leo III. *See* Leo III
Pope Stephen II. *See* Stephen II
Pope Stephen III. *See* Stephen III
Prophet Mohammed, the, 18
Prum, monastery of, 132
public school system, first in Europe, 94
Pyrenees, the, 19, 21, 76, 77-78

Regensburg, palace at, 119, 122
Rhine River, 35, 64, 115, 175
Rhine Valley, 16, 53
Rhone Valley, the, 16
road building, 57
Roland, 78, 80
Roman Empire, 16, 19, 21, 156
Rome, 11, 13, 16, 18, 19, 20, 29, 34, 43-49, 70, 85-86, 89, 108, 115, 142-45, 148-49, 151-52, 157. *See also* Papacy
Romuald, 108-09
Rothaid (daughter) 28, 31, 68
Rotrud (daughter), 68, 139, 172

St. Arnulf's, Church of, 102
St. Boniface, 71, 82
St. Charles, 182
St. Denis, Abbey of, 15, 16, 22, 26, 102, 132
St. Erasmus, monastery of, 144-45
St. Maurice, 12
St. Peter, 156
St. Peter's Church, 46, 49, 145, 152-54
Saragossa, Spain, 76-77
Saxons/Saxony, 18, 35-39, 48, 63-67, 70-72, 74, 82, 99-101, 102-05, 119-20, 145, 165-66, 171, 173
Scandinavia, 149
scriptoria, 97-98, 140
Scotland, 62
serfs, 58, 59
Sigiburg, fortress of, 64
Slavs, 167
Soissons, 22, 96
Song of Roland, 77-80
Spain, 18, 19, 61, 73-78, 113, 119, 121-22, 125, 137
Spoletum, Duchy of, 43, 48-49, 68, 90, 145
Stephen II, 11-16, 19-21